全国职业技能英语系列教材

新编实用汽车英语

主　编　张　伟
副主编　李君梅　钟永发
编　者　周莉琨　罗建芳　杨春秀
　　　　何　玥　邓　锋　李　赟
　　　　徐阳平　陈玛莉

图书在版编目(CIP)数据

新编实用汽车英语/张伟主编;李君梅,钟永发副主编. —北京:北京大学出版社,2011.1
(全国职业技能英语系列教材)
ISBN 978-7-301-18422-6

Ⅰ. ①新… Ⅱ. ①张…②李…③钟… Ⅲ. ①汽车工程－英语－高等学校:技术学校－教材
Ⅳ. ①H31

中国版本图书馆 CIP 数据核字(2011)第 007507 号

书　　　名:	新编实用汽车英语
著作责任者:	张　伟 主编　李君梅　钟永发 副主编
责 任 编 辑:	李　颖
标 准 书 号:	ISBN 978-7-301-18422-6/H・2742
出 版 发 行:	北京大学出版社
地　　　址:	北京市海淀区成府路 205 号　100871
网　　　址:	http://www.pup.cn　电子信箱:zpup@pup.pku.edu.cn
电　　　话:	邮购部 62752015　发行部 62750672　编辑部 62754382　出版部 62754962
印 　 刷 　者:	山东省高唐印刷有限责任公司
经 　 销 　者:	新华书店
	787 毫米×1092 毫米　16 开本　7.75 印张　210 千字
	2011 年 1 月第 1 版　2011 年 1 月第 1 次印刷
定　　　价:	22.00 元

未经许可,不得以任何方式复制或抄袭本书之部分或全部内容。
版权所有,侵权必究
举报电话:(010)62752024　电子信箱:fd@pup.pku.edu.cn

全国职业技能英语系列教材

编委会

顾问

胡壮麟（北京大学）　　　　刘黛琳（中央广播电视大学）

总主编

丁国声（河北外国语职业学院）

编委会名单（以姓氏笔画为序）

丁小莉（山东商业职业学院）
王乃彦（天津对外经济贸易职业学院）
牛　健（中央广播电视大学）
伍忠杰（电子科技大学）
李相敏（河北外国语职业学院）
李恩亮（江苏海事职业技术学院）
张　冰（北京大学出版社）
张九明（开封大学）
张春生（衡水职业技术学院）
陆松岩（江苏城市职业学院）
陈玉华（成都航空职业学院）
林晓琴（重庆电力高等专科学校）
赵　倩（重庆机电职业技术学院）
赵　鹏（北京联合大学）
赵爱萍（浙江水利水电专科学校）
赵翠华（承德民族师范高等专科学校）
胡海青（南京交通职业技术学院）
贾　方（辽宁装备制造职业技术学院）
黄宗英（北京联合大学）
崔秀敏（承德石油高等专科学校）
蒋　磊（河南商业高等专科学校）
程　亚（江西景德镇陶瓷学院）
黎富玉（成都航空职业学院）
潘月洲（南京工业职业技术学院）
Martin Fielko（Cornelsen Press GmbH & Co. KG）

总　序

我国高职高专教育的春天来到了。随着国家对高职高专教育重视程度的加深,职业技能教材体系的建设成为了当务之急。高职高专过去沿用和压缩大学本科教材的时代一去不复返了。

语言学家 Harmer 指出:"如果我们希望学生学到的语言是在真实生活中能够使用的语言,那么在教材编写中接受技能和产出技能的培养也应该像在生活中那样有机地结合在一起。"

教改的关键在教师,教师的关键在教材,教材的关键在理念。我们依据《高职高专教育英语课程教学基本要求》的精神和编者做了大量调查,兼承"实用为主,够用为度,学以致用,触类旁通"的原则,历经两年艰辛,为高职高专学生编写了这套专业技能课和实训课的英语教材。

本套教材的内容贴近工作岗位,突出岗位情景英语,是一套职场英语教材,具有很强的实用性、仿真性、职业性,其特色体现在以下几个方面:

1. 开放性

   本套教材在坚持编写理念、原则及体例的前提下,不断增加新的行业或岗位技能英语分册作为教材的延续。

2. 国际性

   本套教材以国内自编为主,以国外引进为辅,取长补短,浑然一体。目前已从德国引进了某些行业的技能英语教材,还将从德国或他国引进优秀教材经过本土化后奉献给广大师生。

3. 职业性

   本套教材是由高职院校教师与行业专家针对具体工作岗位、情景过程共同设计编写。同时注重与行业资格证书相结合。

4. 任务性

   基于完成某岗位工作任务而需要的英语知识和技能是本套教材的由来与初衷。因此,各分册均以任务型练习为主。

5. 实用性

　　本教材注重基础词汇的复习和专业词汇的补充。适合于在校最后一学期的英语教学，着重培养和训练学生初步具有与其日后职业生涯所必需的英语交际能力。

　　本教材在编写过程中，参考和引用了国内外作者的相关资料，得到了北京大学出版社外语编辑部的倾力奉献，在此，一并向他们表示敬意和感谢。由于本套教材是一种创新和尝试，书中瑕疵必定不少，敬请指正。

丁国声

教育部高职高专英语类专业教学指导委员会委员

河北省高校外语教学研究会副会长

河北外国语职业学院院长

2008 年 6 月

编写说明

随着我国经济发展国际化进程的日益加快,各行业对精通专业技术和具备一定外语能力的复合型人才产生了巨大需求。以汽车工业为例,中国汽车产业已进入快速发展时期。2020年,中国本土汽车产量将达到2000万辆左右,其中两成产品将进入国际市场。中国汽车产业的迅速发展,使得汽车行业对专业技术人员的专业英语水平提出了较之以往的更高要求。尤其在外资或合资企业,与外籍管理人员的沟通涉及大量行业英语的运用。而传统通用型大学英语教材无法满足企业员工对日趋专业化的英语技能的需求。

教育部高等教育司在《高职高专英语课程教学基本要求》中明确提出,高等职业教育不同于一般的学历教育,它培养的是技术、生产、管理、服务等领域的高等应用型专门人才,高等职业教育的基础知识应为培养实际应用能力服务。就英语教学而言,不仅需要注重语言基础知识和基本技能的传授,而且必须突出语言实际应用能力的培养。为了适应汽车行业的发展和市场对该行业从业人员英语水平的要求,配合基础英语的教学,我们编写了这本《实用汽车英语》。它是高级英语阶段的专业英语教材,旨在不断提高汽车类专业学生和汽车行业相关人员的专业英语水平。

本书注重遵循"实用为主,够用为度"、"边学边用,学用结合"的原则,从高职学生的实际情况出发,一方面兼顾汽车专业英语知识学习的系统性,另一方面兼顾基于汽车专业工作过程的知识体系,以汽车构造为主线,注重技能性、突出实用性,加强实训、实践环节,深入浅出地介绍了汽车各主要系统的构造和工作原理,还介绍了汽车维修保养的常识以及常用工具。全书共分为12个单元,每单元前有课前预习,单元后有词汇表、句子注释、练习题和实训内容设计,便于教师教学和学生自学,突出重点、难点,方便学生复习和巩固汽车专业英语知识。每个单元包括课文、配图、词汇、练习等内容,大致分为五个部分:

第一部分为课前预习部分。由浅显易懂的问题和精美的专业图片引入,提高读者阅读兴趣,并能快速把握阅读方向;

第二部分为专业阅读。着重培养学生汽车专业英语的阅读能力。所收入的文章反映了当今汽车专业方面的最新高科技以及最新汽车发展动态，并配以最新的汽车零部件图片展示；课后附有单词、短语，长句、难句的详细注释，提供有课文的参考译文；这些既增强了本书的自学性、阅读性，也降低了教学难度。

第三部分为练习。主要包括专业词汇练习，生词与短语练习，翻译练习、实训内容设计等。设计独特，编排形式新颖，可进一步巩固已学知识。

此外，本书还对英语实用应用文写作知识作了一定的介绍，旨在指导学生了解掌握英语常用应用文写作的方法。

本书图文并茂，内容全面系统，配图清晰精致，难点、重点突出；形式上力求创新，注重实用性和通俗性，真实反映了当代汽车领域发展的前沿技术和最新动态，使学生能够比较系统地掌握汽车方面的英语知识，为其以后阅读、翻译汽车英语资料和操作带有英文标识的仪器、设备等打下坚实的基础。

本书可作为汽车专业的专业英语课程教材，也可作为汽车专业及相关专业工程技术人员提高本专业英语水平的自学读本。

《实用汽车英语》主编为张伟副教授，副主编为李君梅副教授和钟永发副教授，负责全书的统稿与审定；参加编写的教师有周莉琨、罗建芳、杨春秀、何玥、邓锋、李赞，分别负责第一单元、十一单元、十二单元，第二、三单元，第四单元，第五、十单元，第六、七单元，第八、九单元的组稿与编写；英语实用应用文写作部分由张伟、李君梅、徐阳平、陈玛莉编写。此外，本书的编写还得到了四川工程职业技术学院机电工程系汽车检测与维修教研室张仁斌老师的大力帮助，在此表示真诚的感谢。

本教材的编写从内容到形式都有一些新的尝试，限于编者经验和水平，不妥之处，敬请批评指正。同时，鉴于全国各地高职高专院校的实际情况不尽相同，恳请各教学单位在积极选用和推广本教材的同时，注重总结经验，及时提出修改意见和建议，以便再版修订时改正。

编者

2011年1月

CONTENTS

Unit 1　Engine Construction and Operation Principle ·· 1

Unit 2　Fuel System of the Electronically-Controlled Engine ························· 11

Unit 3　Engine Cooling System ·· 21

Unit 4　Engine Lubrication System ··· 33

Unit 5　Clutch ·· 41

Unit 6　Transmission (Including Automatic Transmission) ··························· 49

Unit 7　Steering System ··· 59

Unit 8　Braking System ·· 69

Unit 9　Ignition System ··· 77

Unit 10　Battery, Lights and Signal System ··· 87

Unit 11　Car Maintenance (Ⅰ) ··· 95

Unit 12　Car Maintenance (Ⅱ) ·· 105

Unit 1

Engine Construction and Operation Principle

Warming-up

1. Read the following passage independently with the questions provided below to think about.
   a. Which component is the most important part in an automobile?
   b. How many different types of engines are mentioned in the text according to the number and layout of cylinders?
   c. What is the function of the connecting rod?
   d. On which stroke, the exhaust valve opens and the *piston* moves upward?
2. Write down the relevant terms and expressions in the space provided below.

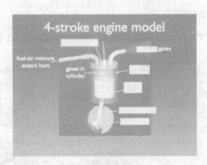

Picture 1

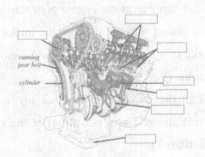

Picture 2

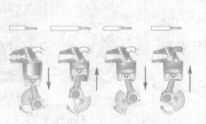

Picture 3

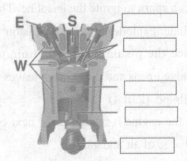

Picture 4

Text

The purpose of a gasoline car engine is to convert gasoline into motion so that your car can move. Currently the easiest way to create motion from gasoline is to burn the gasoline inside an engine. Therefore, a car engine is an internal combustion engine—combustion takes place internally. Two things to note:

- There are different kinds of internal combustion engines. Diesel engines are one form and gas turbine engines are another. Each has its own advantages and disadvantages.
- There is such a thing as an external combustion engine. However, internal combustion is a lot more efficient (takes less fuel per mile) and a lot smaller than external combustion.

Internal Combustion

Almost all cars currently use what is called a four-stroke combustion cycle to convert gasoline into motion. The four strokes are illustrated in Figure 1. They are:

- Intake stroke
- Compression stroke
- Combustion stroke
- Exhaust stroke

You can see in figure 1 that a piston is connected to the crankshaft by a connecting rod. Here's what happens as the engine goes through its cycle:

- The piston starts at the top, the intake valve opens, and the piston moves down to let the engine take in a cylinder full of air and gasoline. This is the intake stroke. (Part 1)
- Then the piston moves back up to compress this fuel/air mixture. Compression makes the explosion more powerful. (Part 2)
- When the piston reaches the top of its stroke, the spark plug emits a spark to ignite the gasoline. The gasoline charge in the cylinder explodes, driving the piston down. (Part 3)
- Once the piston hits the bottom of its stroke, the exhaust valve opens and the exhaust leaves the cylinder to go out the tailpipe. (Part 4)

Now the engine is ready for the next cycle, so it intakes another charge of air and gas.

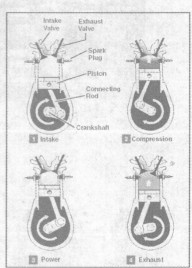

Figure 1

The motion that comes out of an internal combustion engine is rotational. In an engine the linear motion of the pistons is converted into rotational motion by the crankshaft. The rotational motion is nice because we plan to turn (rotate) the car's wheels with it.

Basic Engine Parts

Cylinder

The core of the engine is the cylinder, with the piston moving up and down inside the cylinder. The engine described above has one cylinder. But most cars have more than one cylinder (four, six and eight cylinders are common). In a multi-cylinder engine, the cylinders usually are arranged in one of three ways: inline, V or flat (also known as horizontally opposed or boxer), as shown in the following figures.

Figure 2 Inline–The cylinders are arranged in a line in a single bank.

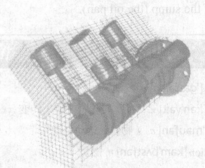

Figure 3 V–The cylinders are arranged at an angle to one another.

Figure 4 Flat–The cylinders are arranged on opposite sides of the engine.

Spark Plug

The spark plug supplies the spark that ignites the air/fuel mixture so that combustion can occur.

Valves

The intake and exhaust valves open at the proper time to let in air and fuel and to let out exhaust. Both valves are closed during compression and combustion so that the combustion chamber is sealed.

Piston

A piston is a cylindrical piece of metal that moves up and down inside the cylinder.

Connecting Rod

The connecting rod connects the piston to the crankshaft. It can rotate at both ends so that its angle can change as the piston moves and the crankshaft rotates.

Crankshaft

The crankshaft turns the piston's up and down motion into circular motion.

Sump

The sump surrounds the crankshaft. It contains some amount of oil, which collects in the bottom of the sump (the oil pan).

New Words

gasoline ['gæsəli:n] n. 汽油
convert [kən'və:t] v.（使）转化，（使）转变
motion ['məuʃən] n.（物体）运动；动作
combustion [kəm'bʌstʃən] n. 燃烧
diesel ['di:z(ə)l] n. 柴油
piston ['pistən] n. 活塞
valve [vælv] n. 气门，阀门

cylinder ['silində] n. 汽缸
explode [ik'spləud] v. 爆炸
tailpipe ['teilpaip] n. 尾气管
rotational [rəu'teiʃənəl] adj. 旋转的
linear ['liniə] adj. 直线的
sump (=the oil pan) [sʌmp] n. 油底壳

Expressions

1. internal combustion engine 内燃机
2. external and internal engine 外燃机
3. gas turbine engine 燃气涡轮发动机
4. intake stroke 进气冲程
5. compression stroke 压缩冲程
6. combustion stroke 做功冲程
7. exhaust stroke 排气冲程
8. spark plug 火花塞
9. connecting rod 连杆

ENGINE CONSTRUCTION AND OPERATION PRINCIPLE   UNIT 1   5

Notes on the Text

1. The purpose of a gasoline car engine is to convert gasoline into motion so that your car can move.

   汽油发动机的目的是将汽油转化成动能来推动汽车移动。

   本句中 to convert... 为不定式作表语；so that 引导目的状语从句，意为"以便，以至于"。

2. However, internal combustion is a lot more efficient (takes less fuel per mile) and a lot smaller than external combustion.

   但是，内燃机比外燃机更加有效（每公里耗油量更少）且更小。

   本句中more...than引导比较状语从句；and连接两个并列成分more efficient和smaller。

3. Almost all cars currently use what is called a four-stroke combustion cycle to convert gasoline into motion.

   几乎现在所有汽车都使用所谓的四冲程循环将汽油转化成动能。

   what 引导宾语从句，to convert ... 为不定式短语作目的状语。

4. It contains some amount of oil, which collects in the bottom of the sump (the oil pan).

   它（油底壳）将油集中在底部。

   which引导非限制性定语从句，先行词为oil。

Exercises

1. Fill in the blanks with the suitable terms according to the text.

| cylinder | exhaust | intake stroke | piston | internal combustion engine |
| spark plug | connecting rod | linear | external combustion | combustion |

(1) A car engine is an _____—combustion takes place internally.

(2) The piston starts at the top, the intake valve opens, and the piston moves down to let the engine take in a cylinder full of air and gasoline. This is _____.

(3) The _____s usually are arranged in one of three ways: inline, V or flat (also known as horizontally opposed or boxer).

(4) The _____ supplies the spark that ignites the air/fuel mixture so that combustion can occur.

(5) The intake and _____ valves open at the proper time to let in air and fuel and to let out exhaust.

(6) The _____ connects the piston to the crankshaft.

(7) In an engine the _____ motion of the pistons is converted into rotational motion by the crankshaft.

(8) However, internal combustion is a lot more efficient (takes less fuel per mile) and a lot smaller than _____.

(9) Once the _____ hits the bottom of its stroke, the exhaust valve opens and the exhaust leaves the cylinder to go out the tailpipe.

(10) Both valves are closed during compression and _____ stroke so that the combustion chamber is sealed.

2. Complete the following sentences with the words and phrases from the passage.

(1) The purpose of a gasoline car engine is to convert _____ into _____ so that your car can move. Currently the easiest way to create motion from gasoline is to burn the gasoline _____ an engine. Therefore, a car engine is an internal combustion engine—combustion takes place internally.

(2) Almost all cars currently use what is called a _____-stroke combustion cycle to convert gasoline into motion.

(3) Once the piston hits the bottom of its stroke, the exhaust valve opens and the exhaust leaves the _____ to go out the _____.

(4) The core of the engine is the cylinder, with the _____ moving up and down inside the cylinder.

(5) There are different kinds of internal combustion engines. _____ engines are one form and _____ turbine engines are another. Each has its own advantages and disadvantages.

3. Match the following English phrases in column A with their Chinese equivalents in Column B.

A	B
exhaust stroke	进气门
engine piston	火花塞
tailpipe	发动机活塞
air-fuel mixture	尾气管
internal combustion engine	排气冲程
spark plug	内燃机
intake valve	可燃混合气

4. Translate the following passages into Chinese.

(1) The motion that comes out of an internal combustion engine is rotational. In an engine the linear motion of the pistons is converted into rotational motion by the crankshaft. The rotational motion is nice because we plan to turn (rotate) the car's wheels with it.

_____

_____

(2) The intake and exhaust valves open at the proper time to let in air and fuel and to let out exhaust. Both valves are closed during compression and combustion so that the combustion chamber is sealed.

_____

_____

5. **Training center practice:**

(1) In a training center, in front of a real engine, students are required to identify the main components and tell their corresponding English terms;

(2) Students are required to introduce the operation principle of an automobile engine by means of indicating the relating parts of the engine.

Learn and Write

Applied Writing: Business Letter

英文书信可分为私人信函和商务信函两大类。私人信函所包含的项目比商务信函少，语言更通俗。商务信函可分为六大部分：

1. 信头（Heading）
(1) 写信的地址、邮政编码、电话、传真号码及电子邮件地址等（Writer's Address）；公司业务用纸上一般印有信头，不必另行再写。
(2) 写信日期（Date）
日期通常有下列两种定法：
（a）月、日、年：如August 15, 2011
（b）日、月、年：如15th august, 2011
2. 信内地址，即收信人的姓名和地址（Inside Address）。
3. 称呼（Salutation）。
称呼指写信人对收信人的称呼，如Dear Xiaojun，写在信头的下方和信笺的左边。称呼一般用Dear...或My dear...开头，称呼后一般用逗号。
4. 正文（Body）。
这是书信的主体部分，即写信人要表达的内容。正文要求文字通顺，层次分明，表意清楚。可以手书，也可以打写。
5. 结束语（Complimentary Close）。
它是书信结尾的恭维话，相当于文中书信最后的"祝好"、"致礼"之类的话语。
6. 签名（Signature）。
签名通常签在结束语下方的中间偏右的位置。签名应是亲笔书写，即使是打印出的信件，最后仍需亲笔签名。在签名的上方可根据写信人和收信人的关系写上Sincerely yours/Yours sincerely（用于长辈或朋友之间），或Respectfully yours/Yours respectfully（用于对长辈或上级）。

Sample

Business Letter Format

Heading ⇒ Sender's Street Address – Number & Street
City   State   Zip
Date

Name of Addressee
Street Address – Number & Street   ⇐ **Inside Address**
City   State   Zip

Dear _____: ⇐ **Greeting**

  As you can tell from the inside address just before the greeting, a business letter is much more formal. This is the type of letter you might write to a company to complain about a product, claim repair or replacement under warranty, **Body** or to request information. The language—grammar and vocabulary—used for this type of writing is very concise and formal. The audience for such a letter needs to be able to read the letter quickly, and understand the message that the writer is sending, whether it is a complaint, a request for information, or some other communication.

The tone of the letter can be as important as its precision. Be sure to communicate your information in a manner appropriate to the situation. For example: register a complaint; don't whine.

Closing ⇒ Sincerely,

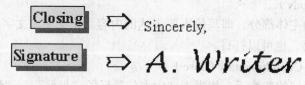

Signature ⇒ *A. Writer*
Type or print your name here

课文译文

发动机的主要构造与工作原理

汽车汽油发动机的目的是将汽油转化成动能用来推动汽车。现在将汽油转化成动能的最简单的方法是在发动机中燃烧汽油。因此,汽车发动机是内燃机——燃烧在内部产生。要注意两点:

- 有不同种类的内燃机。柴油发动机是一种形式,燃气轮机是另一种。每一种都有自身的优势和劣势。
- 还有一种是外燃机。然而,内部燃烧比外部燃烧更加有效(每英里耗油量更少)且小得多。

内燃机

几乎现在所有的汽车都使用一种被称为四冲程的内燃机来将汽油转化成动力。四冲程如图1所示。即:

- 进气冲程
- 压缩冲程
- 做功冲程
- 排气冲程

从图1中可看到活塞通过连杆与曲轴相连。下面是发动机的循环过程:

- 活塞从顶部开始运动,进气门打开,活塞向下运动使发动机汽缸充满可燃混合气。这叫进气冲程。
- 然后活塞向上运动压缩可燃混合气体。压缩使爆发更有力。
- 当活塞到达顶部时,火花塞产生出火花点燃汽油。混合气体在汽缸中爆发出能量,推动活塞向下运动。
- 一旦活塞到达这次冲程末端,排气门打开,废气由汽缸排向排气管。

同时发动机已为下一循环做好了准备,又一次吸入可燃混合气体。

出自内燃机的动力是旋转的。发动机中活塞的线性运动通过曲轴转化成了旋转力。这种旋转力适合于推动旋转的车轮。

主要发动机部件

汽缸

发动机的中心部分就是汽缸,活塞在汽缸中上下运动。上面介绍的发动机有一个汽缸。但是大多数汽车都有不止一个汽缸（四个，六个或八个都很普遍）。在多汽缸发动机中，汽缸通常以三种方式排列：直列，V型或平型（也叫做水平对置式），如下图所示：

火花塞
火花塞提供火花点燃可燃混合气体使燃烧得以发生。

气门
进气门和排气门在适当的时间开合吸入混合气体排出废气。在压缩和做功冲程两处气门都关闭以保证燃烧室的密封状态。

活塞
活塞是在汽缸中上下运动的圆筒状的金属部件。

连杆
连杆连接活塞和曲轴。它两端都能转动，使它的角度能随着活塞的运动和曲轴的转动而改变。

曲轴
曲轴将活塞上下运动转化成旋转的运动。

油底壳
油底壳包围着曲轴。它容纳着聚集在底部的润滑油。

Unit 2

Fuel System of the Electronically-Controlled Engine

Warming-up

1. Read the following passage independently with the questions provided below to think about.
   a. What does a fuel system compose of?
   b. How many types of fuel injections are there?
   c. What is the function of the electronic fuel pump?
   d. What is electronic fuel injection?
2. Write down the relevant terms and expressions in the space provided below.

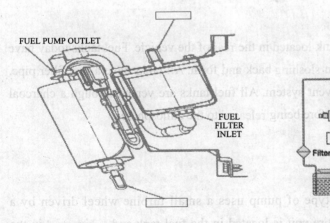

Picture 1

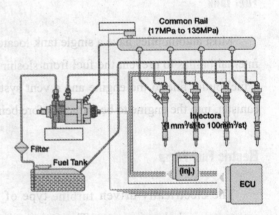

Picture 2

Text

The function of the fuel system is to store and supply fuel to the cylinder chamber where it can be mixed with air, vaporized, and burned to produce energy. The fuel, which can be either gasoline or diesel is stored in a fuel tank. A fuel pump draws the fuel from the tank through fuel lines and delivers it through a fuel filter to either a carburetor or fuel injector, then delivered to the cylinder chamber for combustion.

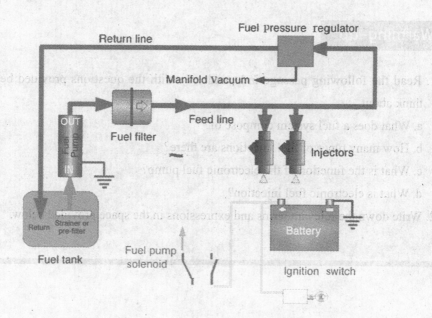

Fuel Tank

Most automobiles have a single tank located in the rear of the vehicle. Fuel tanks today have internal baffles to prevent the fuel from sloshing back and forth. All tanks have a fuel filler pipe, a fuel outlet line to the engine and a vent system. All fuel tanks are vented through a charcoal canister, into the engine to be burned before being released to the atmosphere.

Electric Fuel Pump

The electrically driven turbine type of pump uses a small turbine wheel driven by a constant speed electric motor. The entire unit is located in the fuel tank and submerged in the fuel itself. This pump operates continuously when the engine is running. It keeps up a constant pressure which is capable of supplying the maximum fuel demands of the engine. When less fuel is required, the pump does not deliver at full potential, because the turbine is not a positive displacement type like the mechanical pump. Consequently, the turbine will run without pumping fuel and so it needs no means of varying fuel delivery rate like its mechanical counterpart.

Fuel Filter

The fuel filter is the key to a properly functioning fuel delivery system. Fuel injected cars use electric fuel pumps. When the filter clogs, the electric fuel pump works so hard to push past the filter that it burns itself up. Most cars use two filters. One is inside the gas tank and one in a line to the fuel injectors.

Fuel Line

Steel lines and flexible hoses carry the fuel from the tank to the engine. When servicing or replacing the steel lines, copper or aluminum must never be used. Steel lines must be replaced with steel. When replacing flexible rubber hoses, proper hose must be used. Ordinary rubber such as used in vacuum or water hose will soften and deteriorate.

Electronic Fuel Injection (EFI)

The first fuel injection systems were throttle body fuel injection systems, or single point systems, which had an electrically controlled fuel injector valve. Later, these were replaced by more efficient multi-point fuel injection systems, which have a separate fuel injector for each cylinder. The latter design is better at metering out fuel accurately to each cylinder, and also provides for a faster response.

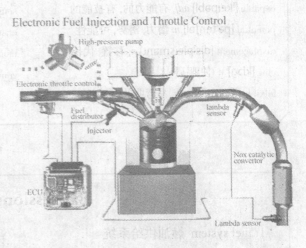

Electronic Fuel Injection and Throttle Control

Although electronic fuel injection is much more complicated than a carburetor, it is much more efficient. The injector is a type of valve that is controlled electronically, which opens and closes and supplies atomized fuel to the engine. It sprays fuel into the intake valves directly in the form of a fine mist. The injector opens and closes rapidly, and the pulse width, or the amount of time it stays open, determines how much fuel goes into the valve. Fuel is supplied to the injectors by a fuel rail.

Several sensors are included as part of the system, to ensure that the correct amount of fuel is delivered to the injectors, and then to the intake valves. These sensors include an engine speed sensor, voltage sensor, coolant temperature sensor, throttle position sensor, oxygen sensor, and airflow sensor. In addition, a manifold absolute pressure sensor monitors the air pressure in the intake manifold to determine the amount of power being generated.

The entire injection system is controlled by an electronic control unit (ECU), which functions as a central exchange for information coming in from all the various sensors. The ECU uses this information to determine the length of pulse, spark advance, and other elements.

New Words

vaporize ['veipəraiz] v. (使)蒸发; (使)汽化
locate [ləu'keit] v. (在……)设置;坐落于
rear [riə] n. 后部, 背
baffle ['bæfl] n. 隔板
slosh [slɔʃ] v. (液体在容器中)晃荡
release [ri'li:s] v. 释放; 放开
turbine ['tə:bin] n. 涡轮机
submerge [səb'mə:dʒ] v. (使)潜入水中, 淹没
capable ['keipəbl] adj. 有能力的, 有技能的
potential [pə'tenʃəl] n. 潜力, 潜势, 可能性
displacement [dis'pleismənt] n. 移置, 代替
clog [klɔg] v. (使)阻碍
felxible ['fleksəbl] adj. 易弯曲的, 柔韧的

service ['sə:vis] v. 检修
replace [ri'pleis] v. 更换, 替换
vacuum ['vækjuəm] n. 真空
deteriorate [di'tiəriəreit] v. 恶化, 变坏
meter ['mi:tə] v. 用仪表测量
atomized ['ætəmaizd] adj. 喷雾状的
spray [sprei] v. 喷
mist [mist] n. 薄雾
sensor ['sensə] n. 传感器, 灵敏元件
ensure [in'ʃuə] v. 确保, 担保
monitor ['mɔnitə] v. 监测, 检测
generate ['dʒenəreit] v. 生成, 产生

Expressions

1. fuel system 燃油供给系统
2. cylinder chamber 气缸
3. fuel tank 燃油箱
4. fuel pump 燃油泵
5. fuel filter 燃油滤清器
6. carburetor 化油器
7. fuel injector 喷油器
8. fuel pressure regulator 油压调节器

FUEL SYSTEM OF THE ELECTRONICALLY-CONTROLLED ENGINE   UNIT 2

9. return line 回油管
10. manifold vaccum 进气岐管
11. feed line 输油管
12. ignition switch 点火开关
13. solenoid 螺线管
14. fuel outlet line 燃油出油管
15. vent system 通风系统
16. charcoal canister 活性炭罐
17. electric motor 电动机
18. mechanical pump 机械泵
19. fuel deliver system 燃油供给系统
20. fuel injection system 燃油喷射系统
21. electric fuel injection 电子燃油喷射
22. electric throttle control 电子控制节气门
23. Nox catalytic converter 氮氧化合物催化转化器
24. multi-point fuel injection system 多点燃油喷射系统
25. intake valve 进气门
26. fuel rail 燃油管
27. engine speed sensor 发动机速度传感器
28. voltage sensor 电压传感器
29. coolant temperature sensor 冷却液温度传感器
30. throttle position sensor 节气门位置传感器
31. oxygen sensor 氧传感器
32. airflow sensor 空气流量传感器
33. manifold absolute pressure sensor 进气岐管绝对压力传感器
34. electric control unit (ECU) 电子控制单元
35. spark advance 提前点火

Notes on the Text

1. The function of the fuel system is to store and supply fuel to the cylinder chamber where it can be mixed with air, vaporized, and burned to produce energy.
   句中where引导一个限制性定语从句，修饰the cylinder chamber。

2. The fuel, which can be either gasoline or diesel, is stored in a fuel tank.

   句中which引导一个非限制性定语从句。

3. The electrically driven turbine type of pump uses a small turbine wheel driven by a constant speed electric motor.

   句中driven by a constant speed electric motor是过去分词短语作后置定语，修饰a small turbine wheel。

4. It keeps up a constant pressure which is capable of supplying the maximum fuel demands of the engine.

   句中which引导一个限制性定语从句，补充说明a constant pressure。

5. When the filter clogs, the electric fuel pump works so hard to push past the filter that it burns itself up.

   句中so... that... 引导结果状语从句，意思是"如此……以至于……"。

6. When servicing or replacing the steel lines, copper or aluminum must never be used.

   句中when servicing or replacing the steel lines是一个省略句，完整应该是when one is servicing or replacing the steel lines. 类似的用法还出现在When replacing flexible rubber hoses, proper hose must be used.

7. The first fuel injection systems were throttle body fuel injection systems, or single point systems, which had an electrically controlled fuel injector valve.

   句中which引导非限制性定语从句，补充说明single point systems。

8. Later, these were replaced by more efficient multi-point fuel injection systems, which have a separate fuel injector for each cylinder.

   句中which引导非限制性定语从句，补充说明multi-point fuel injection systems。

9. The injector is a type of valve that is controlled electronically, which opens and closes and supplies atomized fuel to the engine.

   句中that引导限制性定语从句，修饰a type of valve。句中which引导非限制性定语从句，用来补充说明a type of valve that is controlled electronically。

10. ...and the pulse width, or the amount of time it stays open, determines how much fuel goes into the valve.

    the pulse width, or the amount of time it stays open是句子的主语。句中it stays open是个同位语从句，解释说明the amount of time。

11. The entire injection system is controlled by an electronic control unit (ECU), which functions as a central exchange for information coming in from all the various sensors.

    句中which引导非限制性定语从句，补充说明the electronic control unit。

Exercises

1. Fill in the blanks with the suitable terms according to the text.

the fuel filter	the intake valves	a charcoal canister turbine wheel fuel injector
the air pressure	flexible hoses	fuel injector valve
an electronic control unit		the cylinder chamber

(1) The function of the fuel system is to store and supply fuel to _____ where it can be mixed with air, vaporized, and burned to produce energy.

(2) All fuel tanks are vented through _____, into the engine to be burned before being released to the atmosphere.

(3) The electrically driven turbine type of pump uses a small _____ driven by a constant speed electric motor.

(4) _____ is the key to a properly functioning fuel delivery system.

(5) Steel lines and _____ carry the fuel from the tank to the engine.

(6) The first fuel injection systems were throttle body fuel injection systems, or single point systems, which had an electrically controlled _____.

(7) Later, these were replaced by more efficient multi-point fuel injection systems, which have a separate _____ for each cylinder.

(8) It sprays fuel into directly _____ in the form of a fine mist.

(9) In addition, a manifold absolute pressure sensor monitors _____ in the intake manifold to determine the amount of power being generated.

(10) The entire injection system is controlled by _____, which functions as a central exchange for information coming in from all the various sensors.

2. Complete the following sentences with the words and phrases from the passage.

(1) Most automobiles have a single tank located in _____ of the vehicle. Fuel tanks today have to prevent the fuel from sloshing back and forth.

(2) Consequently, _____ will run without pumping fuel and so, needs no means of varying fuel delivery rate like its mechanical counterpart.

(3) When the filter clogs, _____ works so hard to push past the filter that it burns itself up.

(4) _____ is a type of valve that is controlled electronically, which opens and closes and supplies atomized fuel to the engine.

(5) The ECU uses this information to determine _____, _____ and other elements.

3. Match the following English phrases in column A the Chinese equivalents in Column B.

A	B
vent system	燃油滤清器
fuel filter	电子节气门控制
fuel injector	电子控制装置
electric throttle control	冷却液温度传感器
ignition switch	燃油喷射器
electric control unit (ECU)	通风系统
coolant temperature sensor	点火开关

4. Translate the following passages into Chinese.

(1) When less fuel is required, the pump does not deliver at full potential, because the turbine is not a positive displacement type like the mechanical pump. Consequently, the turbine will run without pumping fuel and so needs no means of varying fuel delivery rate like its mechanical counterpart.

(2) The entire injection system is controlled by an electronic control unit (ECU), which functions as a central exchange for information coming in from all the various sensors.

5. Training center practice:

(1) In a training center, in front of an electronically-controlled engine, students are required to identify the main components of the fuel system and tell their corresponding English terms;

(2) Students are required to introduce the operation principle of fuel system by means of indicating the relating parts of the engine.

课 文 译 文

电控发动燃油系统

燃油供给系统的作用是为气缸存储并给气缸提供燃油，在气缸室里燃油和空气进行混合、气化并燃烧以产生动力。储存在燃油箱中的燃油可以是汽油或者柴油。燃油泵通过燃油输送管将油箱中的燃油吸出并经过燃油滤清器将燃油输送到化油器或是喷油器，然后送到气缸燃烧。

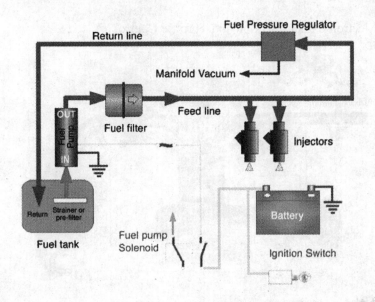

燃油箱

大多数汽车的燃油箱都安装在车尾。现在使用的燃油箱内部都装有隔板防止燃油来回晃荡。所有的燃油箱都装有一根输油管、一根通向发动机的燃油出油管和通风系统。所有的燃油箱都通过活性炭罐通风,然后进入发动机,在排放到空气中之前进行充分的燃烧。

电动燃油泵

电力驱动的涡轮型燃油泵使用一个小的由匀速电动机驱动的涡轮。整个装置安装在燃油箱内并浸泡在燃油中。只要发动机运转,燃油泵就持续工作。燃油泵保持一个稳定的压力,以便为发动机提供所需的最大量燃油。当所需的燃油减少时,燃油泵就不再以最大量提供燃油。因为涡轮机并不像机械泵那样是一种主动的替代装置。因此,涡轮机在没有燃油的情况下仍然运转,所以涡轮机不会像机械泵那样改变燃油输送量。

燃油滤清器

燃油滤清器是燃油供给系统的一个关键的保护装置。燃油喷射汽车使用电动燃油泵。当滤清器阻塞的时候,电动燃油泵就会用力推动燃油绕过滤清器而燃烧起来。大多数汽车都安装了两个滤清器。一个安装在燃油箱内,另一个安装在通向燃油喷射器的油管内。

燃油管

燃油通过钢管和灵活的软管从油箱被输送到发动机。在检修或更换钢管时,决不能使用铜管或是铝管。钢管必须要用钢管来替换。在更换灵活的橡胶软管时,一定要使用合适的软管。普通的橡胶软管或是水管会软化变坏。

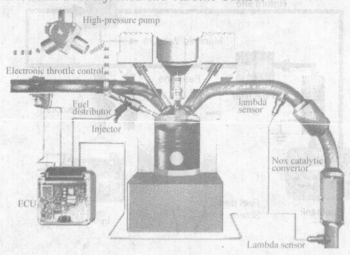

Electronic Fuel Injection and Throttle Control

电子燃油喷射

第一代燃油喷射系统是节气门体燃油喷射系统或者是配有电控燃油喷油器的单点燃油喷射。后来，效率更高的多点燃油喷射取而代之，多点燃油喷射系统使得每个汽缸都有了一个独立的燃油喷油器。这种设计能够更准确地测量每个汽缸需要的燃油，反应也更迅速了。

尽管电子燃油喷射比化油器更复杂，但它的效率更高。喷油器是一种电控的阀门，它打开、闭合并给发动机提供雾化的燃油。它将燃油以微小的雾粒形式喷入进气阀。喷油器快速地打开闭合。它打开的脉冲信号间隙或时间量决定多少燃油进入阀门。燃油通过燃油管供给喷油器。

这个系统还包括几种传感器，确保供给喷油器适量的燃油，然后输送到进气门。这几种传感器包括发动机转速传感器、电压传感器、冷却液温度传感器、节气门位置传感器、氧气传感器以及空气流量传感器。此外，歧管绝对压力传感器监控进气支管内的空气压力，以此来确定产生的动力量。

整个喷射系统是由电子控制装置控制的，它相当于一个信息交换中心，把来自各个传感器的信息进行交换。电子控制装置利用这些信息来确定脉冲的宽度、点火提前角及其他参数。

Unit 3

Engine Cooling System

Warming-up

1. Read the following passage independently with the questions provided below to think about.
   a. What are the main components of engine cooling system?
   b. How many types of engine cooling systems are there?
   c. What features does water-cooling system have?
   d. What are the differences between liquid-cooled system and air-cooled system?
2. Write down the relevant terms and expressions in the space provided below.

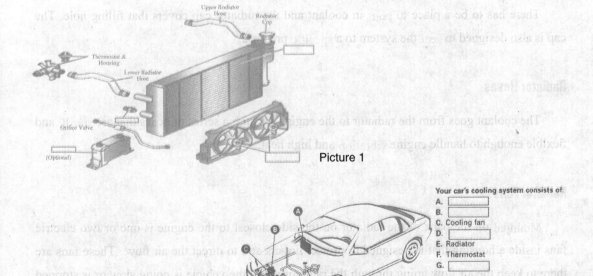

Picture 1

Picture 2

Your car's cooling system consists of:
A.
B.
C. Cooling fan
D.
E. Radiator
F. Thermostat
G.

Text

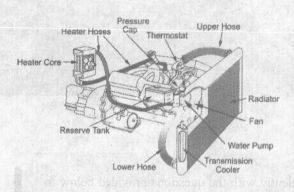

The cooling system is designed to remove heat from the engine to keep the engine operating in its optimal temperature range. If the engine temperature is too low, fuel economy will suffer and emissions will rise. If the temperature is allowed to get too hot for too long, the engine will self destruct. The cooling system is comprised of the following parts:

Radiator

An auto radiator has a set of tubes called the "core" that the coolant flows through. Cooling fins surround the core. As air passes through the fins, the coolant releases its heat to the fins, which dissipate the heat.

Radiator Cap

There has to be a place to pour in coolant and the radiator cap covers that filling hole. The cap is also designed to seal the system to a specific pressure.

Radiator Hoses

The coolant goes from the radiator to the engine through a series of hoses that are sturdy and flexible enough to handle engine vibration and high heat.

Radiator Fans

Mounted on the back of the radiator on the side closest to the engine is one or two electric fans inside a housing that is designed to protect fingers and to direct the air flow. These fans are there to keep the air flow going through the radiator while the vehicle is going slow or is stopped with the engine running.

Water Pump

A water pump is a simple device that will keep the coolant moving as long as the engine is running. It is usually mounted on the front of the engine and turns whenever the engine is running.

Thermostat

The thermostat is simply a valve that measures the temperature of the coolant and, if it is hot enough, opens to allow the coolant to flow through the radiator. If the coolant is not hot enough, the flow to the radiator is blocked and fluid is directed to a bypass system that allows the coolant to return directly back to the engine.

Heater Core

A heater core looks like a small version of a radiator, connected to the cooling system with a pair of rubber hoses. One hose brings hot coolant from the water pump to the heater core and the other hose returns the coolant to the top of the engine. There is usually a heater control valve in one of the hoses to block the flow of coolant into the heater core when maximum air conditioning is called for.

Air-cooled System

The simplest type of cooling is the air-cooled or direct method in which the heat is drawn off by moving air in direct contact with the engine. In air-cooled engines the cylinders are mounted independently to the crankcase so an adequate volume of air can circulate directly around each cylinder, absorbing heat and maintaining cylinder head temperatures within allowable limits for satisfactory operation. In all cases, the cooling action is based on the simple principle that the surrounding air is cooler than the engine. The main components of an air-cooled system are the fan, shroud, baffles, and fins.

Liquid-cooled System

Liquid-cooled system has passages for the liquid, or coolant, through the cylinder block and head. The coolant has to have indirect contact with such engine parts as the combustion chamber, the cylinder walls, and the valve seats and guides. Running through the passages in the engine heats the coolant (it absorbs the heat from the engine parts), and going through the radiator cools it. After getting "cool" again in the radiator, the coolant comes back through the engine. This business continues as long as the engine is running, with the coolant absorbing and removing the engine's heat, and the radiator cooling the coolant.

New Words

remove [ri'mu:v] v. 排除
optimal ['ɔptiməl] adj. 最佳的, 最优的
emission [i'miʃən] n. 排放(物)
comprise [kəm'praiz] v. 组成, 构成
core [kɔ:] n. 核心, 芯
coolant ['ku:lənt] n. 冷冻剂, 冷却液, 散热剂
fin [fin] n. 汽车上的尾翅
release [ri'li:s] v. 释放，排放
dissipate ['disipeit] v. 驱散，消散
pour [pɔ:] v. 涌出
seal [si:l] v. 密封

specific [spi'sifik] adj. 具体的, 特有的, 特定的
sturdy ['stə:di] adj. 强壮的, 结实的
vibration [vai'breiʃən] n. 震动
mount [maunt] v. 安装，镶
measure ['meʒə] v. 量出; 记录
block [blɔk] v. 堵塞, 阻塞
bypass ['baipɑ:s] n. 旁道
crankcase ['kræŋkkeis] n. 曲轴箱
adequate ['ædikwit] adj. 充分的, 足够的
circulate ['sə:kjuleit] v. (使)循环, (使)流通
shroud [ʃraud] n. 遮蔽物; 罩

Expressions

1. cooling system 冷却系统
2. fuel economy 燃油经济性
3. radiator 散热器
4. radiator cap 散热器盖
5. radiator hose 散热器管
6. radiator fan 散热器风扇
7. water pump 水泵
8. thermostat 节温器
9. bypass system 旁通循环
10. heater core 加热器芯
11. air-cooled system 风冷系统
12. liquid-cooled system 水冷系统
13. combustion chamber 燃烧室

Notes on the Text

1. As air passes through the fins, the coolant releases its heat to the fins, which dissipate the heat.
   句中as 引导时间定语从句，意思是"当……的时候"。which引导非限制定语从句，补充说明fins。

2. The coolant goes from the radiator to the engine through a series of hoses that are sturdy and flexible enough to handle engine vibration and high heat.
   句中that引导一个限制性定语从句，修饰限定a series of hoses。

3. Mounted on the back of the radiator on the side closest to the engine is one or two electric fans inside a housing that is designed to protect fingers and to direct the air flow.
   此句是一个倒装句，正常的语序是：one or two electric fans inside a housing that is designed to protect fingers and to direct the air flow is mounted on the back of the radiator on the side closest to the engine. 由于句子的主语过长，为了句子的平衡性，所以使用了倒装。

4. These fans are there to keep the air flow going through the radiator while the vehicle is going slow or is stopped with the engine running.
   句中to keep the air flow going through the radiator 为动词不定式做状语表目的。while 引导时间状语从句，意思是"当……的时候"。with the engine running 是 with引导的独立主格结构，作状语。同样的用法还出现在with the coolant absorbing and removing the engine's heat, and the radiator cooling the coolant。

5. A water pump is a simple device that will keep the coolant moving as long as the engine is running.
   句中that引导限制性定语从句，修饰限定a simple device。as long as 引导条件状语从句，意思是"只要……"。

6. It is usually mounted on the front of the engine and turns whenever the engine is running.
   句中whenever引导时间状语从句。

7. The thermostat is simply a valve that measures the temperature of the coolant and, if it is hot enough, opens to allow the coolant to flow through the radiator.
   句中that引导一个限制性定语从句,修饰a valve。

8. A heater core looks like a small version of a radiator, connected to the cooling system with a pair of rubber hoses.
   句中connected to the cooling system with a pair of rubber hoses是过去分词作后置定语，修饰a radiator。

9. In air-cooled engines the cylinders are mounted independently to the crankcase so an adequate volume of air can circulate directly around each cylinder, absorbing heat and maintaining

cylinder head temperatures within allowable limits for satisfactory operation.

句中so 引导目的状语从句。absorbing heat and maintaining cylinder head temperatures within allowable limits for satisfactory operation 是现在分词作伴随状语。

10. In all cases, the cooling action is based on the simple principle that the surrounding air is cooler than the engine.

句中that引导同位语从句，进一步解释说明the simple principle。

Exercises

1. Fill in the blanks with the suitable terms according to the text.

electric fans	the thermostat	the cooling system	
the radiator cap	liquid-cooled system	a water pump	a heater control valve
the combustion chamber	an air-cooled system	the coolant	

(1) _____ is designed to remove heat from the engine to keep the engine operating in its optimal temperature range.

(2) As air passes through the fins, _____ releases its heat to the fins, which dissipate the heat.

(3) _____ is also designed to seal the system to a specific pressure.

(4) Mounted on the back of the radiator on the side closest to the engine is one or two _____ inside a housing that is designed to protect fingers and to direct the air flow.

(5) _____ is a simple device that will keep the coolant moving as long as the engine is running.

(6) _____ is simply a valve that measures the temperature of the coolant.

(7) There is usually _____ in one of the hoses to block the flow of coolant into the heater core when maximum air conditioning is called for.

(8) The main components of _____ are the fan, shroud, baffles, and fins.

(9) _____ has passages for the liquid, or coolant, through the cylinder block and head.

(10) The coolant has to have indirect contact with such engine parts as _____, the cylinder walls, and the valve seats and guides.

2. Complete the following sentences with the words and phrases from the passage.

(1) An auto _____ has a set of tubes called the "core" that the _____ flows through.

(2) As air passes through _____, the coolant releases _____ to the fins, which dissipate the heat.

(3) If the coolant is not hot enough, the flow to the radiator is blocked and fluid is directed to _____ that allows the coolant to return directly back to _____.

(4) _____ looks like a small version of a radiator, connected to _____ with a pair of rubber hoses. One hose brings hot coolant from _____ to the heater core and the other hose returns the coolant to the top of the engine.

(5) In air-cooled engines _____ are mounted independently to the crankcase so an adequate volume of air can circulate directly around each cylinder, absorbing _____ and maintaining cylinder head temperatures within allowable limits for satisfactory operation.

3. Match the following English phrases in column A the Chinese equivalents in Column B.

A	B
cooling system	燃油经济性
thermostat	冷却风扇
air-cooled system	水冷系统
radiator	节温器
fuel economy	冷却系统
liquid-cooled system	散热器
cooling fan	风冷系统

4. Translate the following passages into Chinese.

(1) If the coolant is not hot enough, the flow to the radiator is blocked and fluid is directed to a bypass system that allows the coolant to return directly back to the engine.

_____
_____

(2) After getting "cool" again in the radiator, the coolant comes back through the engine. This business continues as long as the engine is running, with the coolant absorbing and removing the engine's heat, and the radiator cooling the coolant.

_____
_____

5. Training center practice:

(1) In a training center, in front of an engine, students are required to point out the main parts of the cooling system in English

(2) Students are required to introduce the operation principle of the cooling system by means of indicating the relating parts of the engine.

Learn and Write

Applied Writing: Invitation Card

请柬（Invitation Cards）一般分为正式和非正式两种。正式请柬的特点是：格式比较规范，用词准确、简洁。非正式请柬就可以是熟人之间比较随便的便条了。

正式请柬一般包括的内容有：宾主姓名（邀请人与被邀请人姓名）、表示欢迎的句子、聚会内容、时间（具体到日、时、分，还要有星期几）、地点，如果需要的话，还有特别说明的文字。英语请柬中的邀请套用语"Request the pleasure of the company of"，相当于汉语中的"敬请光临"。

需要注意的是：

1. 宾主姓名一律采用第三人称，其中人名、单位名、节日和活动名称都应采用全称。夫妇同时具名时，通常"先生"写在其"夫人"前。行文不用标点符号。

2. 时间不用阿拉伯数字写。写请柬的日期一般不写在请柬上。需安排座位的宴请活动，应要求被邀者答复能否出席。请柬上一般注上R.S.V.P.（请答复）法文缩写字样，并注明联系电话，也可用电话询问能否出席。

3. 若邀请人对被邀者出席时的服装有要求，可在请柬的左下角或右下角加以注明。请柬一般提前一周至二周发出。

Sample 1

谨定于2010年12月11日(星期六)下午3点在牛津街圣彼得教堂为小女南希和爱德华·索尔斯基先生举行婚礼。敬请威廉斯先生和夫人光临。

格林教授和夫人鞠躬

敬请赐复

Professor and Ms. Green

request the pleasure of the company of

Mr. and Mrs. Williams

on the occasion of the marriage of their daughter

Nancy

to Mr. Edward Solski

at St. Peter's Church, Oxbridge

on Saturday, the eleventh of December, 2010

at 3:00 p. m.

R.S.V.P

Sample 2

　　谨定于2011年4月23日（星期六）下午6时在柳树大街布里奇酒家举行宴会，欢迎原子能研究所高级工程师刘文凌先生。
敬请迪肯森先生和夫人光临
原子弹研究所所长谨订
如不能出席,请赐复为盼
电话：8880784
衣着：听便

Director of the Institute of Atomic Energy
requests the pleasure of the company of Mr. and Mrs. Dickens
at a dinner party
in honor of Mr. Liu Wenling
senior engineer of the Institute of Atomic Energy
on Saturday, April 23, 2011
at six o'clock p.m.
at Bridge Restaurant in Willow Avenue

Reply if declining　　Dress: Informal
Tel: 8880784

课文译文

发动机冷却系统

　　冷却系统的作用是释放发动机产生的热能从而保证发动机在最佳的温度范围。如果发动机的温度过低，燃油经济性就受影响，尾气排放就会增加。如果发动机长时间保持高温，发动机就会受损。冷却系统主要由以下几个部分组成：

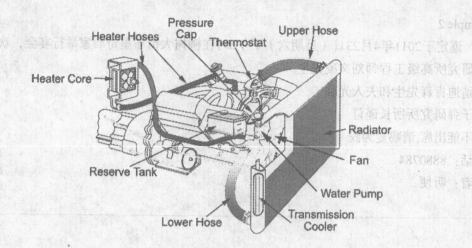

散热器

汽车的散热器是由一组被称为"芯"的管道构成的,冷却液在这些管道中流动。冷却翼片包围着这个芯。当空气通过翼片时,冷却液就把热能释放到翼片,驱散热气。

散热器盖

汽车都必须有一个可以注入冷却液的孔,散热器盖就是用来盖住注液孔的。散热器盖还用来密封冷却系统使其保持特定的压力。

散热器管

冷却液通过一系列软管从散热器流到发动机。这些软管要足够的结实灵活可以抗发动机的震动和高温。

散热器扇

在最靠近发动机的散热器后面安装着一台或两台电控风扇,风扇有个外壳用来保护并引流。当汽车慢速行驶或发动机怠速时,这些风扇保证气流正常通过散热器。

水泵

水泵是一种保证发动机运转时冷却液在流动的简单装置。它通常安装在发动机的前面,只要发动机运转,它就旋转。

节温器

节温器是一种简单地测量冷却液温度的阀门。如果节温器温度很高时,就会打开使冷却液流到散热器。如果冷却液温度不高,流向散热器的液体就受阻而流到旁通系统,使得冷却液直接回流到发动机。

加热器芯

加热器芯看上去就像一个小型的散热器，它由一对橡胶软管连接到冷却系统。其中一根软管将水泵中高温的冷却液带到加热器芯，而另一根软管将冷却液返回到汽缸盖。在其中的一根软管中通常都安装有一个加热器控制阀，在需要最大化的空气调控时阻止冷却液流入加热器芯。

风冷系统

最简单的冷却类型就是风冷，它是一种通过空气流动直接从发动机吸取热能的方法。在风冷发动内，气缸独立安装在曲轴箱内，因此在每个气缸内有足够的空气进行循环，吸收热能并将气缸内的温度保持在允许的范围内，确保发动机正常运转。无论在哪种情况下，冷却方法都是建立在一个简单的原理之上，即周围的空气温度要低于发动机的温度。风冷系统的主要组成部分有：风扇、冷却罩、隔板以及翼片。

水冷系统

水冷系统配有液体或冷却液流动到气缸体和气缸盖的通道。发动机的组成部分，如燃烧室、汽缸壁以及气门座和气门导管等间接地连接冷却液。流过发动机的通道时就加热冷却液（它从发动机的各部分吸收热能），流过散热器时就将其冷却。在散热器内再一次"冷却"后，冷却液又流回到发动机。只要发动机旋转，这一过程就会一直持续下去，冷却液吸收并释放发动机的热能，然后散热器再次将其冷却。

Unit 4

Engine Lubrication System

Warming-up

1. Read the following passage independently with the questions provided below to think about.
   a. What is the function of the lubrication system?
   b. What are the main components of the lubrication system?
   c. How is the oil circulated in the engine parts?
   d. What are the main lubrication methods?
2. Write down the relevant terms and expressions in the space provided below.

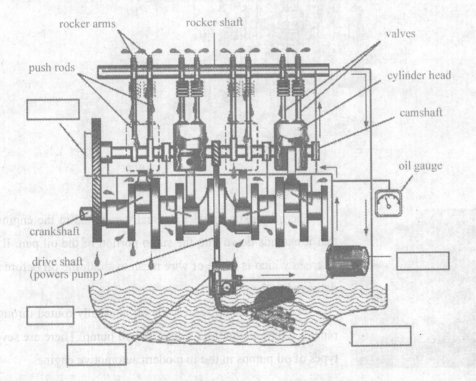

Text

Function of Engine Lubrication System

The engine lubrication system supplies oil to all the friction surfaces between the engine moving parts. If the lubrication system did not supply these moving components with oil, friction would quickly destroy these surfaces. The oil reduces friction between moving component, which increases engine power and efficiency. Engine components are lubricated, cooled, cleaned, and sealed by the oil in the lubrication system. The oil also reduces wear on engine components to a minimum. The purpose of the lubrication system is to circulate oil between moving engine parts. Oil between the parts prevents metal-to-metal contact which causes friction and wear.

Lubrication System Components

The reservoir for storing the oil is known as the oil pan. Most oil pans, especially on military wheeled vehicles, have a fairly deep section known as the sump.

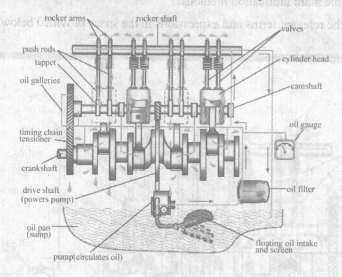

The oil pickup or inlet is usually mounted in the engine so that it extends down into the sump portion of the oil pan. It has a screen which is made of wire mesh to strain the oil before it is delivered to the pump.

From the pickup screen, the oil is usually routed through a pipe or a tube to the inlet side of the oil pump. There are several types of oil pumps in use in modern automotive engines.

ENGINE LUBRICATION SYSTEM UNIT 4   35

Depending on the method used to pump the oil, the pumps are called gear, vane, rotor, or plunger types. The gear and rotor types are the most commonly used in automotive engines.

An oil pressure relief valve is usually placed in the main oil line (also known as the oil gallery) leading from the pump or built into the discharge side of the pump itself.

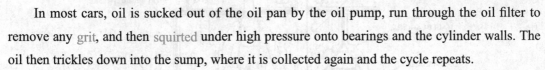

An oil filter is used in the lubrication system to remove all the abrasive materials possible.

In most cars, oil is sucked out of the oil pan by the oil pump, run through the oil filter to remove any grit, and then squirted under high pressure onto bearings and the cylinder walls. The oil then trickles down into the sump, where it is collected again and the cycle repeats.

Lubrication Methods

There are three types of lubrication systems used in internal combustion engines. They are the splash, the combination splash and force-feed.

On the splash system there is a dipper on the bottom of the connecting rod. This dipper splashes the oil all over the inside of the engine. All of the moving parts are lubricated by the oil splashed on them by the dipper.

An engine using the combination splash and force-feed systems of engine lubrication still relies on dippers on the connecting rods to lubricate the connecting rod journals, the cylinder walls, and the pistons and rings. Other parts, such as the main bearings, valves, camshaft, and timing gears are lubricated by oil supplied by a pressure pump.

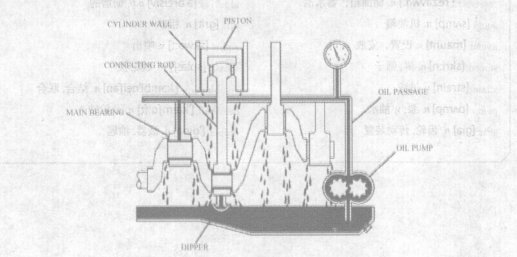

On the force-feed lubrication system, there are no dippers on the connecting rods. Instead, the crankshaft has drilled passageways leading from each of the main bearing journals to the connecting rod journals. Oil is delivered to the main bearing by the pump. Part of the oil travels through the drilled passageways to the connecting rod journals.

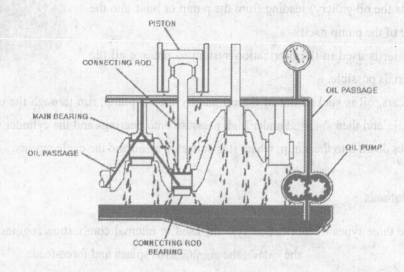

New Words

lubrication [ˌluːbrɪˈkeɪʃən] n. 润滑油	vane [veɪn] n. 叶片
friction [ˈfrɪkʃən] n. 摩擦	rotor [ˈrəʊtə] n. 转子，回转轴
seal [siːl] v. 密封	plunger [ˈplʌndʒə] n. 活塞
minimum [ˈmɪnɪməm] n. 最小值，最小化	discharge [dɪsˈtʃɑːdʒ] v. 流出，释放
circulate [ˈsɜːkjʊleɪt] v. 循环	filter [ˈfɪltə] n. 滤清器，过滤器
reservoir [ˈrezəvwɑː] n. 储油箱，蓄水池	abrasive [əˈbreɪsɪv] adj. 研磨的
sump [sʌmp] n. 机油箱	grit [grɪt] n. 粗砂
mount [maʊnt] v. 设置，安放	squirt [skwɜːt] v. 喷出
screen [skriːn] n. 屏，筛子	splash [splæʃ] v. 飞溅，泼
strain [streɪn] v. 过滤	combination [ˌkɒmbɪˈneɪʃən] n. 结合，联合
pump [pʌmp] n. 泵; v. 抽水	camshaft [ˈkæmʃɑːft] n. 凸轮轴
gear [gɪə] n. 齿轮，传动装置	dipper [ˈdɪpə] n. 汲器，油匙

ENGINE LUBRICATION SYSTEM　UNIT 4

Expressions

1. engine lubrication system　发动机润滑系统
2. friction surfaces　摩擦面
3. oil pan　油底壳
4. oil pickup　机油集滤器
5. wire mesh　金属网眼
6. oil pressure relief valve　限压阀
7. main oil line　主油道
8. oil gallery　主油道
9. suck out　吸出
10. trickle down　滴落
11. combination splash and force feed system　飞溅和压力结合式润滑
12. force feed system　压力润滑
13. connecting rod　连接杆
14. cylinder wall　汽缸壁
15. main bearing　主轴承
16. pressure pump　压力泵

Notes on the Text

1. If the lubrication system did not supply these moving components with oil, friction would quickly destroy these surfaces.
   如果没有润滑系的供油，这些表面很快就会由于摩擦而损毁。句中if 引导条件状语从句。

2. Engine components are lubricated, cooled, cleaned, and sealed by the oil in the lubrication system.
   润滑系统中润滑油对发动机部件起到润滑、散热、清洗及密封等作用。句中谓语动词为一般现在时态的被动语态。

3. The oil pickup or inlet is usually mounted in the engine so that it extends down into the sump portion of the oil pan.
   机油集滤器通常安装在发动机上使其可以延伸到油底壳的机油箱部分。句中so that 引导目的状语从句。

4. An oil pressure relief valve is usually placed in the main oil line (also known as the oil gallery) leading from the pump or built into the discharge side of the pump itself.
   限压阀通常安装在油泵通向主油道的地方或是油泵的出口方。

5. On the force-feed lubrication system, there are no dippers on the connecting rods. Instead, the crankshaft has drilled passageways leading from each of the main bearing journals to the connecting rod journals.

压力润滑系统中，连接杆上不再有油匙。而是在机轴上钻出从主轴承头到连接杆的油道。

Exercises

1. Fill in the blanks with the suitable terms according to the text.

pressure pump	oil pressure relief valve	oil pump	oil filter
oil pan	dipper	oil pickup or inlet	connecting rod
drilled passageways	friction		

(1) The engine lubrication system supplies oil to all the _____ surfaces between the engine moving parts.

(2) The reservoir for storing the oil is known as the _____.

(3) The _____ is usually mounted in the engine so that it extends down into the sump portion of the oil pan.

(4) An _____ is usually placed in the main oil line (also known as the oil gallery).

(5) An _____ is used in the lubrication system to remove all the abrasive materials possible.

(6) In most cars, oil is sucked out of the oil pan by the _____.

(7) On the splash system there is a _____ on the bottom of the connecting rod.

(8) Other parts, such as the main bearings, valves, camshaft, and timing gears are lubricated by oil supplied by a _____.

(9) Instead, the crankshaft has _____ leading from each of the main bearing journals to the connecting rod journals.

(10) On the splash system there is a dipper on the bottom of the _____.

2. Complete the following sentences with the words and phrases from the passage.

(1) The engine _____ supplies oil to all the friction surfaces between the engine moving parts.

(2) Engine components are _____, _____, _____, and _____ by the oil in the lubrication system.

(3) Oil between the parts prevents _____ which causes friction and wear.

(4) From the _____, the oil is usually routed through a pipe or a tube to the _____ of the oil pump.

(5) Depending on the method used to pump the oil, the pumps are called _____, vane, _____, or plunger types.

3. Match the following English phrases in column A the Chinese equivalents in Column B.

A	B
force-feed system	油底壳
oil pressure relief valve	飞溅润滑
oil pickup	压力泵
splash lubrication	压力润滑
pressure pump	限压阀
oil pan	机油集滤器

4. Translate the following passages into Chinese.

(1) Engine components are lubricated, cooled, cleaned, and sealed by the oil in the lubrication system. The oil also reduces wear on engine components to a minimum.
_____
_____

(2) The oil pickup or inlet is usually mounted in the engine so that it extends down into the sump portion of the oil pan. It has a screen which is made of wire mesh to strain the oil before it is delivered to the pump.
_____
_____

5. Training center practice:

(1) In a training center, in front of a real engine, students are required to identify the main components of the lubrication system and tell their corresponding English terms;

(2) Students are required to introduce the lubrication process by means of indicating the relating parts of the engine.

课 文 译 文

发动机润滑系统

润滑系的作用

发动机润滑系向发动机主要运动部件的摩擦表面提供机油。如果没有润滑系的供油，这些表面很快就会由于摩擦而损毁。润滑油能减少运动部件之间的摩擦，从而提高发动机的功率和效率。润滑系中润滑油对发动机部件起到润滑、散热、清洗及密封等作用，还将发动机部件的磨损降到最低。润滑系的功能就是使机油在发动机部件之间循环,防止部件间直接接触产生摩擦和损耗。

润滑系的组成

储存机油的容器叫做作油底壳。多数油底壳,特别是在军用车辆上,有一个相当深的部分被称为机油箱。机油集滤器通常安装在发动机上使其可以延伸到油底壳的机油箱部分,它有一个由金属网眼做成的筛子,使机油在进入油泵之前得到过滤。从机油集滤器吸取上来的机油沿着管道进入油泵的人口处。现代汽车发动机常使用的油泵主要有几种类型,根据泵油的方式分为齿轮式、叶片式、转子式和活塞式,齿轮式和转子式是最常见的类型。限压阀通常安装在油泵通向主油道的地方或是油泵的出口方。机油滤清器主要用来用来过滤掉润滑油中的磨屑。在大多数的汽车中,润滑油通过油泵从油底壳中被抽出,流经机油滤清器去除细小杂质,再被高压喷射到轴承和汽缸壁上,然后滴落到机油箱中,再次被收集起来,而下一个循环又开始了。

润滑方式

内燃机主要有三种润滑方式:飞溅润滑,飞溅和压力结合式润滑和压力润滑。

在飞溅润滑系统中,在连接杆的底部有一个油匙,他可以使机油飞溅到发动机内部,从而使所有运动部件都可以得到润滑。

使用飞溅和压力结合式润滑的发动机仍然使用油匙来润滑连接杆轴颈、汽缸壁、活塞和活塞环等,其他部件,比如主轴承、阀门、凸轮轴和齿轮则由压力泵所供的油进行润滑。

压力润滑系统中,连接杆上不再有油匙。而是在机轴上钻出从主轴承头到连接杆的油道。通过油泵向主轴输出润滑油。部分润滑油经由油路到达连接杆。

Unit 5 Clutch

Warming-up

1. Read the following passage independently with the questions provided below to think about.
   a. Where is the clutch installed?
   b. How many basic parts does a clutch have? And what are they?
   c. What are the functions of the clutch?
   d. List the types of clutch spring.
2. Write down the relevant terms and expressions you know about these pictures.

Picture 1

Picture 2

Text

A clutch is a component of an engine's transmission designed to allow engagement or disengagement of the engine to whatever apparatus is being driven. When a vehicle is to be moved from rest the clutch must engage a stationary gearbox shaft with the engine; this must be rotating at a high speed to provide sufficient power or else the load will be too great and the engine will stall (come to rest).

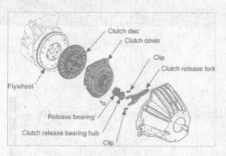

The clutch has three main functions: Firstly, provides a smooth take-up of the drive. And, it can disengage the drive when necessary. The third function is preventing the overload of power train

The clutch is composed of four basic parts: driving members, driven members, pressing mechanisms and operating members.

Driving Member

The driving member consists of two parts: the flywheel and the pressure plate. The flywheel is bolted directly to the engine crankshaft and rotates when the crankshaft turns. The pressure plate is bolted to the flywheel. The result is that both flywheel and pressure plate rotate together.

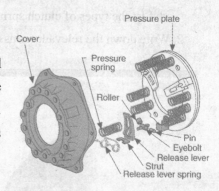

Driven Member

The driven member, or clutch disc, is located between the flywheel and pressure plate. The disc has a splined hub that locks to the splined input shaft on the gearbox. Any rotation of the clutch disc turns the input shaft.

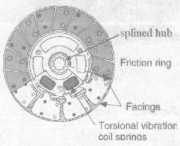

The inner part of the clutch disc, called the hub flange, has a number of small coil springs. These springs are called torsional springs. They let the middle part of the clutch disc turn slightly on the hub. Thus, the springs absorb the torsional vibrations of the crankshaft. When the springs have compressed completely, the clutch moves back until the springs relax. In other words, the clutch absorbs these engine vibrations, preventing the vibrations from going through the drive train.

Operating Members

These are the parts that release pressure from the clutch disc. The operating members consist of the clutch pedal, clutch return spring, clutch linkage, clutch fork, and release bearing. The clutch linkage includes the clutch pedal and a mechanical or hydraulic system to move the other operating members.

When the clutch pedal is depressed, the clutch linkage operates the clutch fork. The clutch fork, or release fork, moves the release bearing against the pressure plate release levers. These levers then compress springs that normally hold the clutch disc tightly against the flywheel.

When the clutch pedal is released, the pressure plate forces the clutch disc against the flywheel. The clutch return spring helps raise the pedal.

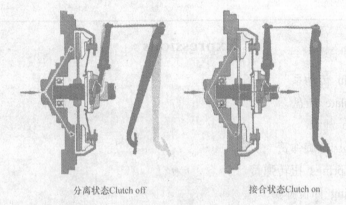

分离状态Clutch off   接合状态Clutch on

离合器操纵示意图
Sketch of clutch controlling

Hopefully it's becoming clear why the DCT（Dual Clutch Transmission，双离合变速）is classified as an automated manual transmission. In principle, the DCT behaves just like a standard manual transmission: It's got input and auxiliary shafts to house gears, synchronizers and a clutch. What it doesn't have is a clutch pedal, because computers, solenoids and hydraulics do the actual shifting. Even without a clutch pedal, the driver can still "tell" the computer when to take action through paddles, buttons or a gearshift.

It certainly offers smooth acceleration by eliminating the shift shock that accompanies gearshifts in manual transmissions and even some automatics. Best of all, it affords drivers the luxury of choosing whether they prefer to control the shifting or let the computer do all of the work.

Perhaps the most compelling advantage of a DCT is improved fuel economy. Because power flow from the engine to the transmission is not interrupted, fuel efficiency increases dramatically. Some experts say that a six-speed DCT can deliver up to a 10 percent increase in relative fuel efficiency when compared to a conventional five-speed automatic.

New Words

component [kəm'pəunənt] n. 成分 adj. 组成的，构成的

engagement [in'geidʒmənt] n. 接合

disengagement ['disin'geidʒmənt] n. 脱离

apparatus [ˌæpə'reitəs] n. 器械，设备，仪器

stationary ['steiʃ(ə)nəri] adj. 固定的

bolt [bəult] n. 螺钉，闪电 v. 上门闩，用螺丝上

spline [splain] n. 花键 vt. 用花键联接，开键槽

vibration [vai'breiʃən] n. 振动，颤动，摇动，摆动

mechanical [mi'kænikl] adj. 机械的，机械制的，机械似的；呆板的

hydraulic [hai'drɔ:lik] adj. 水力的，液压的

pedal ['pedl] n. 踏板 v. 踩……的踏板

Expressions

1. power train 传动系
2. pressure plate 压盘
3. hub flange 毂缘
4. coil springs 螺旋弹簧
5. torsional springs 扭转弹簧
6. return spring 回位弹簧
7. clutch fork 离合器分离叉
8. release bearing 分离弹簧
9. release lever 分离杆

Notes on the Text

1. When a vehicle is to be moved from rest the clutch must engage a stationary gearbox shaft with the engine; this must be rotating at a high speed to provide sufficient power or else the load will be too great and the engine will stall (come to rest).

   这句话中，when 引导的句子做时间状语，句中 this 代指 engine，or else 的意思是"否则"。stall 的意思是"熄火"。

2. The flywheel is bolted directly to the engine crankshaft and rotates when the crankshaft turns.

   be bolted to "被上在"。

   这句话的意思是"飞轮用螺栓直接连接到发动机曲轴上，随曲轴旋转而旋转"。

3. The driven member, or clutch disc, is located between the flywheel and pressure plate. The disc has a splined hub that locks to the splined input shaft on the gearbox.

   be located 后加介词，意思是"位于……"。input shaft, 输入轴。这句话的意思是从动部分（或从动盘）位于飞轮和压盘之间。从动盘上有花键毂，连接着变速器上带花键的输入轴。

4. When the springs have compressed completely, the clutch moves back until the springs relax.

   be compressed, "被……压缩"。relax,指弹簧"伸张"。

5. In other words, the clutch absorbs these engine vibrations, prevents the vibrations from going through the drive train.

   In other words, 换句话说。后面的absorb 与 prevent 引导的两个动宾结构是两个并列的句子成分。

   也就是说，离合器吸收发动机的振动，防止振动传递给传动系。

Exercises

1. Fill in the blanks with the suitable terms according to the text.

engagement	disengagement	take-up	power train
driving members	operating members	flywheel	pressure plate
clutch return spring	release bearing		

(1) A clutch is a subcomponent of an engine's transmission designed to allow _____ or _____ of the engine to whatever apparatus is being driven.

(2) The clutch has three main functions: Firstly, provides a smooth _____ of the drive. And, it can disengage the drive when necessary. The third function is preventing the overload of _____.

(3) The clutch is composed of four basic parts: _____, driven members, pressing mechanisms and _____.

(4) The driven member, or clutch disc, is located between the _____ and _____.

(5) The operating members consist of the clutch pedal, _____, clutch linkage, clutch fork, and _____.

2. Complete the following sentences with the words and phrases from the passage.

(1) When the _____ is released, the pressure plate forces the clutch disc against the flywheel. The clutch _____ helps raise the pedal.

(2) _____ are the parts that release pressure from the clutch disc.

(3) _____, or clutch disc, is located between the flywheel and pressure plate.

(4) When a vehicle is to be moved from rest the _____ must engage a stationary gearbox shaft with the engine _____.

(5) _____ is bolted directly to the engine crankshaft and rotates when the crankshaft turns.

3. **Match the following English phrases in column A the Chinese equivalents in Column B.**

A	B
clutch fork	离合器片
pressure plate	主动部件
driving members	离合器分离叉
torsional springs	压盘
clutch disc	扭转弹簧
flywheel	离合器盖
clutch cover	飞轮

4. **Translate the following passages into Chinese.**

(1) The inner part of the clutch disc, called the hub flange, has a number of small coil springs. These springs are called torsional springs. They let the middle part of the clutch disc turn slightly on the hub.

_____

_____

(2) When the clutch pedal is depressed, the clutch linkage operates the clutch fork. The clutch fork, or release fork, moves the release bearing against the pressure plate release levers. These levers then compress springs that normally hold the clutch disc tightly against the flywheel.

_____

_____

5. **Training center practice:**

(1) In a training center, in front of a real clutch, students are required to identify the main components and tell their corresponding English terms;

(2) Students are required to introduce the operation principle of an automobile clutch by means of indicating the relating parts of the power train.

Learn and Write

Applied Writing: English Envelope

英文信封的写法

```
┌─────────────────────────────────────────────────────────┐
│  (Sender)                                       ┌─────┐ │
│  Ming Li                                        │STAMP│ │
│  23, Lane130,                                   └─────┘ │
│  Sec.Ⅱ Nanking East Rd.                                 │
│  Deyang, Si Chuan 618000                                │
│  China                                                  │
│                                                         │
│                                                         │
│                              (Addressee)                │
│                              Mr. George Wang            │
│                              1025 Long Street,          │
│                              San Francisco, CA 94101    │
│                              U.S.A.                     │
└─────────────────────────────────────────────────────────┘
```

1. 在信封的左上角写寄信人的名字和住址。

2. 在信封的中间或右下角偏左的地方写收信人的名字和住址。

3. 寄信人不自称Mr., Mrs.或Miss，但是在收信人的姓名前则必须加上尊称Mr., Mrs.或Miss以示礼貌。

4. 住址的写法与中文相反；英文住址原则上是由小至大，如必须先写门牌号码、街路名称，再写城市、省（州）和邮政区号，最后一行则写上国家的名称。

5. 在信封的右上角贴上邮票。

6. 信封上的邮政区号(zip code)，在美国州名之后以五位数阿拉伯数字表示，前三位数代表州或都市，后两位数表示邮区，至于邮政区号10027的念法是one double o two seven。

7. 住址中常用字(有简写的多用简写)：

楼 Floor (e.g. 2F)

巷 Lane (e.g. Lane 194)

段 Section；Sec. (e.g. Sec.Ⅱ)

路 Road；Rd. (e.g. Chunhua Rd.)

街 Street；St. (e.g. Yangwang St.)

课文译文

离合器

离合器是发动机传动系统中的一个基础部件,无论什么样的发动机,传动系都可以接上或是脱开。当汽车原地起步时,离合器要将静止的变速器轴同发动机接合起来,此时发动机必须高速旋转以提供足够大的功率,否则载荷过大将引起发动机熄火。

离合器有三个主要功能:首先,提供平稳的起步。其次,在必要的时候切断传动系。第三个功能是防止传动系过载。

离合器由四个基本部分组成:主动部件、从动部件、压紧装置和操纵部件。

主动部分

主动部分由飞轮和压盘两部件组成。飞轮用螺栓直接连接到发动机曲轴上,随曲轴旋转而旋转。压盘与飞轮连接,这样飞轮和压盘一起旋转。

从动部分

从动部分(或从动盘)位于飞轮和压盘之间。从动盘上有花键毂,连接着变速器上带花键的输入轴。从动盘的旋转带动变速器输入轴随之转动。

从动盘的内侧(毂缘)有一些叫做扭转弹簧的小螺旋弹簧,这些弹簧使得从动盘中部相对从动盘毂能有轻微转动,从而吸收曲轴的扭转振动。压紧弹簧完全压缩时,离合器向后移动直到弹簧开始伸张为止。也就是说,离合器吸收发动机的振动,防止振动传递给传动系。

操纵部件

操纵部件是从离合器盘上释放压力的零部件。操纵部件包括离合器踏板、离合器回位弹簧、离合器杆、离合器叉及分离轴承。离合器杆包括离合器踏板及机械或是液压系统,从而移动操纵部件的其他部分。

踩下离合器踏板,离合器杆系操纵分离叉。分离叉带动分离轴承压向压盘上的分离杠杆,分离杠杆压缩压紧弹簧。通常情况下,压紧弹簧使从动盘和飞轮紧密接合。

释放离合器踏板,压盘使从动盘同飞轮接合,回位弹簧使离合器踏板抬起。

人们越来越清楚为什么DCT的被列为手自一体。从基本原理上来看,DCT表现为标准手动传动:它有输入和辅助轴安置齿轮、同步装置和传动器。它不具备的是离合器踏板,因为电脑,螺线管和水力系统替它完成工作。即使没有离合器踏板,司机也可以通过阀门,按钮或者是变速器"告诉"电脑什么时候采取行动。

它通过消除手动变速器和一些自动变速器带来的换挡停滞,为汽车提供平稳加速。最棒的是,它使司机能够随地选择是自己控制加速或让电脑来完成所有工作。

也许一个DCT的最引人注目的优点是提高燃油经济性。由于从发动机到变速器的功率传输不会中断,因此燃油效率大大增加。一些专家称,与传统的五速自动变速箱相比,一个6速DCT的可以将燃油率提高10%。

Unit 6

Transmission (Including Automatic Transmission)

Warming-up

1. Read the following passage independently with the questions provided below to think about.
   a. What is transmission? And what is automatic transmission?
   b. How many types of automatic transmission are there? And what are they?
   c. What is the function of transmission?
   d. What are the advantages of continuously variable transmission over traditional automatic transmission?
2. Write down the relevant terms and expressions in the space provided below.

Picture 1

Picture 2

Picture 3

Picture 4

Text

Transmission, also called transmission gear box, is one of the most principle parts of the drive system in motor cars. Made up of drive machinery and gear-shift machinery, transmission is a gear drive device to fix or change gears at the transmission ratio of the output shaft and the input shaft. Meanwhile the motor car transmission changes the torque by altering the transmission ratio, to adapt to the needs of different requirements to drive wheels traction and speed under different driving conditions, such as starting, acceleration, driving, and overcoming all kinds of road obstacles.

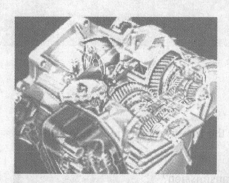
Transmission

Operation Principle and Function

Transmission consists of variable-speed transmission structures and variable-speed control structures. The main function of variable-speed transmission structures is to change the numerical value and the direction of torque and rev; and the main role of variable-speed control structures is to control the transmission structures, to realize the transformation of transmission ratio, that is, to realize gear shifting, so as to achieve speed change and torque variation. Transmission has the following four functions:

(1) To change transmission ratio to meet the need for traction under different road conditions, meanwhile to make the engine as far as possible in favorable conditions to satisfy the requirements for possible driving speed.

(2) To realize driving astern for satisfying the need of vehicle's regressive driving. Engine crankshaft generally rotates in one direction only, but vehicles sometimes need to be able to drive astern. Therefore, people usually tend to use the reverse gear set in the gear box to realize driving astern.

(3) To interrupt the transmission of power, or to interrupt power transmission to wheel when starts engine, operates in idle speed, shifts gear or needs parking for power output.

(4) To realize a neutral gear so that the gear box will not output power when the clutch engages. For example, it can ensure driver to release the clutch pedal and to leave his car without switching off the motor.

Classification

Generally Transmission is classified into manual transmission (MT), automatic transmission (AT), manual/automatic transmission, and continuously variable transmission (CVT).

MT

Manual transmission, also called manual shift, usually refers to changing transmission ratio only through changing the location of gear meshing in transmission by hand, so as to achieve the purpose of speed change. Only when pedal down the clutch, can the gear lever be moved. Manual / automatic transmission means that it is set with choice of "+" and "–" on the stalls of the car. When on the D stall, driver can freely change lower stall "–" or higher stall "+", as on manual transmission.

AT

Continuously variable transmission is composed of two sets of ratio gears and a power belt. Therefore, it is simpler in structure and smaller in bulk than traditional automatic transmission. In addition, it can change the transmission ratio freely to achieve full infinite variable speed so that to change the vehicle's speed smoothly. CVT is also a kind of automatic transmission.

Automatic Transmission

Automatic transmission, which can change speed automatically according to the degree of the accelerator pedal and the speed changes, effects the speed change by gear mechanism, so drivers only need manipulate the accelerator pedal to control speed. It has the advantages of easy manipulation, comfortable driving and being able to reduce drivers' fatigue. There are three common types of automatic transmission: hydraulic automatic transmission (AT), machinery continuously variable transmission (CVT), and automated mechanical transmission (AMT). At present, AT is widely used in cars, and it almost becomes a synonym of automatic transmission. AT consists of torque converter, epicycle gear and hydraulic control system. It usually

CVT

achieves speed change and torque variation through hydraulic transmission and gear combination, among which torque converter is the most important component. Torque converter is composed of components of pump impeller, turbine, and guide pulley and so on. It has the function of both transmission of torque and clutch.

New Words

transmission [trænz'miʃən] n. 变速器
gear-shift [giə-ʃift] n. 齿轮换挡
Meanwhile ['mi:n,hwail] adv. 同时
torque [tɔ:k] n. 转矩
adapt [ə'dæpt] v. (使)适应, (使)适合
traction ['trækʃən] n. 拖, 拉, 牵引；牵引动力
acceleration [æk,selə'reiʃən] n. 加速
obstacle ['ɔbstəkl] n. 障碍(物), 妨碍
variable-speed ['vɛəriəbl-spi:d] n. 变速
numerical [nju:'merikəl] adj. 数字的, 用数字表示的, 数值的
rev [rev] n. 一次回转,(每分钟的)转速
transformation [,trænsfə'meiʃən] n. 变化, 弯形, 变质, 转变
favorable ['feiərəbl] adj. 有利的, 良好的
satisfy ['sætisfai] v. 使满意; 满足
astern [əs'tə:n] adv. 向后
crankshaft ['kræŋkʃa:ft] n. 机轴

rotate [rəu'teit] v. (使某物)旋转[转动]
reverse [ri'və:s] adj. 相反的, 颠倒的, 反向的
interrupt [,intə'rʌpt] v. 打断
idle ['aidl] adj. 空闲的, 闲着的
neutral ['nju:trəl] n. (汽车或其他机器的)空挡位置
engage [in'geidʒ] v. 吸引, 占用; vt. & vi. (使)从事于, (使)忙于
release [ri'li:s] v. 释放; 放开
mesh [meʃ] v. (使)啮合, 钓住(with); 使密切配合
lever ['li:və] n. 操作杆
stall [stɔ:l] n. 档位
compose [kəm'pəuz] v. 组成, 构成
bulk [bʌlk] n. 体积
manipulate [mə'nipjuleit] v. 熟练控制[操作]
fatigue [fə'ti:g] n. 疲劳, 劳累
synonym ['sinənim] n. 代名词
component [kəm'pəunənt] n. 成分, 组成部分, 部件, 元件

Expressions

1. transmission gear box 变速箱
2. gear drive device 齿轮传动装置
3. output shaft 输出轴;从动轴
4. input shaft 输入轴
5. transmission ratio 传动比
6. variable-speed transmission structures 变速传动机构
7. variable-speed control structures 变速操纵机构
8. gear shifting 换档
9. torque variation 变矩
10. the reverse gear 倒档
11. neutral gear 空档

12. clutch pedal 离合器踏板
13. manual transmission (MT) 手动变速器
14. automatic transmission (AT) 自动变速器
15. manual / automatic transmission 手动/自动变速器
16. continuously variable transmission (CVT) 无级变速器
17. gear meshing 齿轮啮合
18. the gear lever 变速杆
19. ratio gear 变速轮盘
20. power belt 传动带
21. infinite variable speed 无级变速
22. the accelerator pedal (汽车等的)加速踏板
23. torque converter 液力变扭器
24. epicycle gear 行星齿轮
25. hydraulic control system 液压操纵系统
26. pump impeller 泵轮
27. guide pulley 导轮

Notes on the Text

1. Meanwhile the motor car transmission changes the torque by altering the transmission ratio, to adapt to the needs of different requirements to drive wheels traction and speed under different driving conditions, such as starting, acceleration, driving, and overcoming all kinds of road obstacles.

   而汽车变速器是通过改变传动比,而改变转矩，适应在起步、加速、行驶以及克服各种道路阻碍等不同行驶条件下对驱动车轮牵引力及车速不同要求的需要。

   句中such as 表示比例说明，后跟名词。如用for example，后面须跟分句。

2. ...and the main role of variable-speed control structures is to control the transmission structures, to realize the transformation of transmission ratio, that is, to realize gear shifting, so as to achieve speed change and torque variation.

   变速操纵机构的主要作用是控制传动机构，实现变速器传动比的变换，即实现换档，以达到变速变矩。

   句中that is是一个插入语；so as to引导出的是目的状语。

3. Only when pedal down the clutch, can the gear lever be moved.

踩下离合器时，方可拨得动变速杆。

当出现Only, hardly, seldom副词在句首时，句子须部分倒装。

4. Automatic transmission, which can change speed automatically according to the degree of the accelerator pedal and the speed changes, effect the speed change by gear mechanism, so drivers only need manipulate the accelerator pedal to control speed.

自动变速器利用齿轮机构进行变速，它能根据油门踏板的程度和车速变化，自动地进行变速，而驾驶者只需操纵加速踏板控制车速即可。

句中which引导出的是一个非限制性定语从句。

5. It usually achieves speed change and torque variation through hydraulic transmission and gear combination, among which torque converter is the most important component.

AT是由液力变扭器、行星齿轮和液压操纵系统组成，通过液力传递和齿轮组合的方式来达到变速变矩。其中液力变扭器是AT最重要的部件。

Exercises

1. Fill in the blanks with the suitable terms according to the text.

neutral gear	manual shift	the transmission ratio	infinite variable speed
torque and rev	torque variation	transmission gear box	the gear lever
epicycle gear	engine crankshaft		

(1) Transmission is a gear drive device to fix or change gears at _____ of the output shaft and the input shaft.

(2) _____ generally rotates in one direction only, but vehicles sometimes need to be able to drive astern.

(3) Transmission, also called _____, is one of the most principle parts of the drive system in motor cars.

(4) To realize a _____ so that the gear box will not output power when the clutch engages.

(5) Manual transmission, also called _____, usually refers to changing transmission ratio only through changing the location of gear meshing in transmission by hand.

(6) AT consists of torque converter, _____ and hydraulic control system.

(7) In addition, it can change the transmission ratio freely to achieve full _____ so that to change the vehicle's speed smoothly.

(8) It usually achieves speed change and _____ through hydraulic transmission and

gear combination.

(9) Only when pedal down the clutch, can _____ be moved.

(10) The main function of variable-speed transmission structures is to change the numerical value and the direction of _____.

2. Complete the following sentences with the words and phrases from the passage.

(1) Automatic transmission, which can change speed _____ according to the _____ of the accelerator pedal and the speed changes, _____ the speed change by gear mechanism, so driver only need manipulate the _____ to control speed.

(2) AT consists of _____, _____ and _____.

(3) Transmission changes the torque by altering the _____, to adapt to the needs of different requirements to drive _____ and speed under different driving conditions, such as starting, _____, driving, and overcoming all kinds of _____.

(4) Generally Transmission is classified into _____, _____, _____, and _____.

(5) Automatic transmission has the advantages of _____, _____ and _____.

3. Match the following English phrases in column A the Chinese equivalents in Column B.

A	B
torque variation	无级变速器
neutral gear	离合器踏板
torque converter	无级变速
continuously variable transmission (CVT)	空档
the gear lever	泵轮
clutch pedal	变速杆
pump impeller	变矩
infinite variable speed	液力变扭器

4. Translate the following passages into Chinese.

(1) At present, AT is widely used in cars, and it almost becomes a synonym of automatic transmission. AT consists of torque converter, epicycle gear and hydraulic control system. It usually achieves speed change and torque variation through hydraulic transmission and gear combination, among which torque converter is the most important component.

_____

_____

(2) Continuously variable transmission is composed of two sets of ratio gears and a power belt. Therefore, it is simpler in structure and smaller in bulk than traditional automatic transmission.

_____

_____

5. Training center practice:

(1) In a training center, students are required to identify different kinds of transmission and to talk about the differences between them;

(2) Students are required to check the main parts of AT and tell about its advantages in English.

课 文 译 文

变速器（含自动变速器）

变速器又称变速箱是汽车传动系中最主要的部件之一。变速器由传动机构和变速机构组成,是能改变输出轴和输入轴传动比的齿轮传动装置。汽车变速器是通过改变传动比,而改变转矩,适应在起步、加速、行驶以及克服各种道路阻碍等不同行驶条件下对驱动车轮牵引力及车速不同要求的需要。

工作原理及功能

变速器由变速传动机构和变速操纵机构两部分组成。变速传动机构的主要作用是改变转矩和转速的数值和方向；变速操纵机构的主要作用是控制传动机构,实现变速器传动比的变换,即实现换档,以达到变速变矩。变速器有如下四个功能：

(1) 改变传动比，满足不同行驶条件对牵引力的需要，使发动机尽量工作在有利的工况下，满足可能的行驶速度要求。

(2) 实现倒车行驶，用来满足汽车倒退行驶的需要。发动机曲轴一般都是只能向一个方向转动的，而汽车有时需要能倒退行驶，因此，往往利用变速箱中设置的倒档来实现汽车倒车行驶。

(3) 中断动力传递，在发动机起动，怠速运转，汽车换档或需要停车进行动力输出时，中断向驱动轮的动力传递。

(4) 实现空档，当离合器接合时，变速箱可以不输出动力。例如，可以保证驾驶员在发动机不熄火时松开离合器踏板离开驾驶员座位。

分类

通俗上分为手动变速器(MT),自动变速器(AT),手动/自动变速器，无级式变速器(CVT)等。

手动变速器，也称手动档，即用手拨动变速杆才能改变变速器内的齿轮啮合位置，改变传动比，从而达到变速的目的。踩下离合器时，方可拨得动变速杆；手动/自动变速器是指在车的档位上设有"+"、"-"选择档位。在D档时，可自由变换降档(-)或加档(+)，如同手动档一样；无级变速器是由两组变速轮盘和一条传动带组成的。因此，要比传统自动变速器结构简单，体积更小。另外，它可以自由改变传动比，从而实现全程无级变速，使汽车的车速变化平稳。无级变速器属于自动变速器的一种。

自动变速器

自动变速器利用齿轮机构进行变速，它能根据油门踏板程度和车速变化，自动地进行变速，而驾驶者只需操纵加速踏板控制车速即可。自动变速器具有操作容易、驾驶舒适、能减少驾驶者疲劳的优点。汽车自动变速器常见的有三种类型：分别是液力自动变速器(AT)、机械无级自动变速器(CVT)、电控机械自动变速器(AMT)。目前轿车普遍使用的是AT，AT几乎成为自动变速器的代名词。AT是由液力变扭器、行星齿轮和液压操纵系统组成，通过液力传递和齿轮组合的方式来达到变速变矩。其中液力变扭器是AT最重要的部件，它由泵轮、涡轮和导轮等构件组成，兼有传递扭矩和离合的作用。

Unit 7

Steering System

Warming-up

1. Read the following passage independently with the questions provided below to think about.
   a. What is the definition of steering system?
   b. What is mechanical steering system, and what is power steering system?
   c. What is the full spelling of EPS?
   d. How many kinds of steering mechanism are there? What are they?
2. Write down the relevant terms and expressions in the space provided below.

Picture 1

Picture 2

Picture 3

Picture 4

Text

The mechanism used to change or maintain the driving direction of cars is called steering system. The function of automotive steering system is to control the driving directions according to drivers' wishes. Automotive steering system is essential to driving safety.

Steering System

Classification and Operation Principle

Automotive steering system is divided into two types: mechanical steering system, and power steering system.

Mechanical steering system

The steering system entirely manipulated by driver is known as the mechanical steering system. Mechanical steering system takes driver's physical force as energy of direction shift. All transmission parts in it are mechanical. The three main kinds of steering control mechanism, steering gear and steering linkage mechanism comprise the mechanical steering system.

(1) Steering control mechanism

Steering control mechanism consists of steering wheel, steering shaft, steering column and other components. Its function is to pass driver's operation force on rotation of steering wheel to steering gear.

(2) Steering gear

Steering gear (also called steering booster) is a set of gear mechanism that completing the process of moving from rotary motion to rectilinear motion. It is also the creeper gear of steering system.

Steering gear

(3) Steering linkage mechanism

The function of steering linkage mechanism is to turn the force and motion output by the steering gear towards steering joint on both sides of steering axle, thus to deflect the steering wheels on both sides, and to make the deflection angles of two steering wheels change according to certain relationship, therefore to ensure that the relative sliding between wheels and ground is as small as possible when cars change directions.

The use of mechanical steering device can achieve speed changing of cars. When the steering shaft is overloaded, it is not easy to change speed only by the use of driver's physical force as energy of direction shift. The steering system manipulated by dynamic force is called power steering system. It is formed by adding a set of steering booster devices on the basis of mechanical steering system. Power steering system can also be divided into hydraulic power steering system and electric power steering system.

(1) Hydraulic power steering system

When drivers turn the steering wheel, they will move the tie rod through mechanical steering, and then drive the knuckle arm to make the steering wheel deflect, and thus to change the car's driving directions. At the same time, the steering gear input shaft will also drive the steering control valve within the steering gear to rotate, so to make the power cylinder generate hydraulic force to help driver manipulate direction changes. As a result of steering booster device, driver can make the steering wheel deflect simply by much smaller steering torque than that of mechanical steering system.

(2) Electric power steering system

Electric power steering system is named electric EPS or EPS for short. It adds signal sensors, electronic control units and steering booster devices on the basis of mechanical steering devices. Electric EPS utilizes motor as its power source, and completes power control under the help of electronic control units according to the factors of speed and steering parameters. The principle can be summarized as follows: When manipulating the steering wheel, the torque transducer installed in the steering wheel axis continuously measure the shift signal on torque axis, and then the signal and speed signal will be input into the electronic control units at the same time. Electronic control units will then make sure the size and direction of power toque according to these input signals, that is to say, to select the current and rotational directions of motor and adjust the size of steering auxiliary power. Motor torque will be added to the steering mechanism on the car after adding torque by decelerated through reducing mechanism of the electromagnetic clutch, so that it can gain a steering force adaptable to the car's working conditions.

EPS

New Words

mechanism ['mekənizəm] n. 机械装置, 机构, 机制
essential [i'senʃəl] adj. 至关重要的
mechanical [mi'kænikəl] adj. 机械的
entirely [in'taiəli] adv. 全部地，完全地
column ['kɔləm] n. 柱状物
booster ['bu:stə] n. 助力[推]器，加速器
rotary ['rəutəri] adj. 旋转的
rectilinear [,rekti'liniə] adj. 直线的
joint [dʒɔint] n. 节
axle ['æksl] n. 轴
deflection [di'flekʃən] n. 偏转
ensure [in'ʃuə] v. 确定，确保
sliding ['slaidiŋ] adj. 滑动的
overload [,əuvə'ləud] v. 使超载

dynamic [dai'næmik] adj. 动力的，动态的
basis ['beisis] n. 基础
knuckle ['nʌkl] n. 转向节
signal ['signəl] n. 信号
utilize ['ju:tilaiz] v. 利用
factor ['fæktə] n. 因素
parameter [pə'ræmitə] n. 参数
summarize ['sʌməraiz] v. 概括，总结，摘要
transducer [trænz'dju:sə] n. 传感器
install [in'stɔ:l] v. 安装
axis ['æksis] n. 轴，轴线
current ['kʌrənt] n. 电流
auxiliary [ɔ:g'ziljəri] adj. 辅助的
electromagnetic [i,lektrəumæg'netik] adj. 电磁的

Expressions

1. automotive steering system 汽车转向系统
2. mechanical steering system 机械转向系统
3. power steering system 动力转向系统
4. physical force 体力
5. steering control mechanism 转向操纵机构
6. steering gear 转向器
7. steering linkage mechanism 转向传动机构
8. steering wheel 方向盘
9. steering shaft 转向轴
10. steering column 转向管柱
11. operation force 操纵力
12. rotary motion 旋转运动
13. rectilinear motion 直线运动
14. creeper gear 减速传动装置

15. steering joint 转向节
16. the deflection angle 偏转角
17. steering axle 转向桥
18. hydraulic power steering system 液压式动力转向系统
19. electric power steering system 电动助力动力转向系统
20. dynamic force 动力
21. the tie rod 横拉杆
22. power cylinder 转向动力缸
23. steering booster device 转向加力装置
24. steering torque 转向力矩
25. power source 助力源
26. steering auxiliary power 转向辅助动力
27. electromagnetic clutch 电磁离合器

Notes on the Text

1. The mechanism used to change or maintain the driving direction of cars is called steering system.
   用来改变或保持汽车行驶方向的机构称为汽车转向系统。
   句中used to 用作定语，前面省略了which is。

2. Mechanical steering system takes driver's physical force as energy of direction shift. All transmission parts in it are mechanical.
   机械转向系统以驾驶员的体力作为转向能源，其中所有传力件都是机械的。
   句中takes...as表示"将……当作……"。

3. Steering gear (also called steering booster) is a set of gear mechanism that completing the process of moving from rotary motion to rectilinear motion.
   转向器(也常称为转向机)是完成由旋转运动到直线运动(或近似直线运动)的一组齿轮机构。
   句中that引导出的是定语从句。

4. When the steering shaft is overloaded, it is not easy to change speed only by the use of driver's physical force as energy of direction shift.
   当转向轴负荷较大时，仅靠驾驶员的体力作为转向能源则难以顺利转向。

句中when引导出的是一个条件状语从句。

5. It is formed by adding a set of steering booster devices on the basis of mechanical steering system.
动力转向系统就是在机械转向系统的基础上加设一套转向加力装置而形成的。
这是一个被动句。

Exercises

1. Fill in the blanks with the suitable terms according to the text.

steering axle	power toque	the steering control valve	power control
the tie rod	the electromagnetic clutch		the driving directions
steering control mechanism		dynamic force	steering booster device

(1) The function of automotive steering system is to control _____ according to drivers' wishes.

(2) The function of _____ is to pass driver's operation force on rotation of steering wheel to steering gear.

(3) The function of steering linkage mechanism is to turn the force and motion output by the steering gear towards steering joint on both sides of _____.

(4) Electric EPS utilizes motor as its power source, and completes _____ under the help of electronic control units.

(5) Electronic control units will then make sure the size and direction of _____ according to these input signals.

(6) When drivers turn the steering wheel, they will move _____ through mechanical steering.

(7) The steering system manipulated by _____ is called power steering system.

(8) At the same time, the steering gear input shaft will also drive _____ within the steering gear to rotate.

(9) As a result of _____, driver can make the steering wheel deflect simply by much smaller steering torque than that of mechanical steering system.

(10) Motor torque will be added to the steering mechanism on the car after adding torque by decelerated through reducing mechanism of _____.

2. Complete the following sentences with the words and phrases from the passage.

(1) The function of steering linkage mechanism is to turn the force and motion output by the

_____ towards _____ on both sides of _____.

(2) When manipulating the steering wheel, the _____ installed in the _____ continuously measure the shift signal on torque axis.

(3) Electric power steering system is named _____ or _____ for short.

(4) Power steering system can also be divided into _____ and _____.

(5) Steering control mechanism consists of _____, _____, _____ and other components.

3. Match the following English phrases in column A the Chinese equivalents in Column B.

A	B
operation force	机械转向系统
steering control mechanism	直线运动
power cylinder	减速传动装置
steering axle	转向辅助动力
steering auxiliary power	转向动力缸
rectilinear motion	转向操纵机构
mechanical steering system	操纵力
creeper gear	转向桥

4. Translate the following passages into Chinese.

(1) The three main kinds of steering control mechanism, steering gear and steering linkage mechanism comprise the mechanical steering system.
_____
_____

(2) It adds signal sensors, electronic control units and steering booster devices on the basis of mechanical steering devices. Electric EPS utilizes motor as its power source, and completes power control under the help of electronic control units according to the factors of speed and steering parameters.
_____
_____

5. Training center practice:

(1) In a training center, students are required to tell what is mechanical steering system, and what is power steering system;

(2) Students are required to make a conclusion to the principle of EPS.

Learn and Write

Applied Writing: Résumé

个人简历

Sample

Résumé

Name: *Sun Yang*

Address: *108 Taishan Road Deyang Sichuan 618000*

Date of Birth: *March 3, 1975*

Sex: *Female*

Marital status: *Single*

Health: *Excellent*

Education:

1985—1991 No.1 Middle School, Deyang, Sichuan Province

1991—1995 Sichuan Normal University, Chengdu, Sichuan Province

        Major: *English*

        Received B.A. in English, July 1995

Work experience:

1994   *Translator and guide for foreign athletes*

1995—present *Teacher of English*

        Foreign Language Department, Sichuan Engineering and Technical College

Awards and Scholarships:

1985—1991   "Excellent Student", No.1 Middle School

1991—1995   Recipient of university scholarships, Sichuan Normal University

Interests: *Travel, swimming, playing guitar*

References: *Available upon request*

---

1. 标题

个人简历多用"个人简历"、"求职简历"作标题。

2. 正文

正文有一段式和多段式两种结构方法。

（1）一段式：从姓名、诞生地、籍贯、出生年月、民族、团体党派写起，按时间顺序叙述主要学习、工作经历，主要成绩、贡献。

（2）多段式：适用于经历较丰富，年岁较大的人。写法是：先总述主要经历，再分段叙述各阶段或各方面主要经历。

写个人简历要求是：不夸大不缩小，概括集中，语言朴素，真实可信。

课文译文

转向系统

用来改变或保持汽车行驶方向的机构称为汽车转向系统。汽车转向系统的功能就是按照驾驶员的意愿控制汽车的行驶方向。汽车转向系统对汽车的行驶安全至关重要。

分类及工作原理

汽车转向系统分为两大类：机械转向系统和动力转向系统。

完全靠驾驶员手力操纵的转向系统称为机械转向系统。机械转向系统以驾驶员的体力作为转向能源，其中所有传力件都是机械的。机械转向系统由转向操纵机构、转向器和转向传动机构三大部分组成。

（1）转向操纵机构

转向操纵机构由方向盘、转向轴、转向管柱等组成，它的作用是将驾驶员转动转向盘的操纵力传给转向器。

（2）转向器

转向器(也常称为转向机)是完成由旋转运动到直线运动(或近似直线运动)的一组齿轮机构，同时也是转向系中的减速传动装置。

（3）转向传动机构

转向传动机构的功用是将转向器输出的力和运动传到转向桥两侧的转向节，使两侧转向轮偏转，且使二转向轮偏转角按一定关系变化，以保证汽车转向时车轮与地面的相对滑动尽可能小。

使用机械转向装置可以实现汽车转向，当转向轴负荷较大时，仅靠驾驶员的体力作为转向能源则难以顺利转向。借助动力来操纵的转向系统称为动力转向系统。动力转向系统就是在机械转向系统的基础上加设一套转向加力装置而形成的。动力转向系统又可分为液压动力转向系统和电动助力动力转向系统。

（1）液压式动力转向系统

当驾驶员转动转向盘时，通过机械转向器使转向横拉杆移动，并带动转向节臂，使转向轮偏转，从而改变汽车的行驶方向。与此同时，转向器输入轴还带动转向器内部的转向控制阀转动，使转向动力缸产生液压作用力，帮助驾驶员转向操作。由于有转向加力装置的作用，驾驶员只需比采用机械转向系统时小得多的转向力，就能使转向轮偏转。

（2）电动助力动力转向系统

简称电动式EPS或EPS。它是在机械转向机构的基础上，增加信号传感器、电子控制单元和转向助力机构。电动式EPS是利用电动机作为助力源，根据车速和转向参数等因素，由电子控制单元完成助力控制，其原理可概括如下：当操纵转向盘时，装在转向盘轴上的转矩传感器不断地测出转向轴上的转矩信号，该信号与车速信号同时输入到电子控制单元。电控单元根据这些输入信号，确定助力转矩的大小和方向，即选定电动机的电流和转动方向，调整转向辅助动力的大小。电动机的转矩由电磁离合器通过减速机构减速增矩后，加在汽车的转向机构上，使之得到一个与汽车工况相适应的转向作用力。

Unit 8 Braking System

Warming-up

1. Read the following passage independently with the questions provided below to think about.
   a. What is the other name of the anti-lock brake controller?
   b. How many different parts does an ABS consist of?
   c. What does ECU stand for?
   d. If a fault develops in any part of the ABS, what kind of response will take place?
2. Write down the relevant terms and expressions in the space provided below.

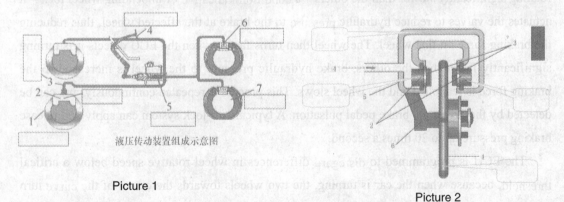

液压传动装置组成示意图

Picture 1

Picture 2

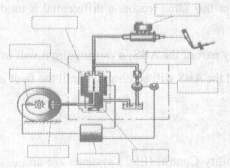

Picture 3

--- *Text* ---

Modern ABS

In 1975, Robert Bosch took over a European company called Teldix (contraction of Telefunken and Bendix) and all the patents registered by this joint-venture and took advantage out of this acquisition to build the base of the system introduced on the market some years later. The German firms Bosch and Mercedes-Benz had been co-developing anti-lock braking technology since the 1970s, and introduced the first completely electronic 4-wheel multi-channel ABS system in trucks and the Mercedes-Benz S-Class in 1978. ABS Systems based on this more modern Mercedes design were later introduced on other cars and on motorcycles.

Operation

The anti-lock brake controller is also known as the CAB (Controller Anti-lock Brake).

A typical ABS is composed of a central electronic control unit (ECU), four wheel speed sensors—one for each wheel—and two or more hydraulic valves within the brake hydraulics. The ECU constantly monitors the rotational speed of each wheel, and when it detects a wheel rotating significantly slower than the others—a condition indicative of impending wheel lock—it actuates the valves to reduce hydraulic pressure to the brake at the affected wheel, thus reducing the braking force on that wheel. The wheel then turns faster; when the ECU detects it is turning significantly faster than the others, brake hydraulic pressure to the wheel is increased so the braking force is reapplied and the wheel slows. This process is repeated continuously, and can be detected by the driver via brake pedal pulsation. A typical anti-lock system can apply and release braking pressure up to 20 times a second.

The ECU is programmed to disregard differences in wheel rotative speed below a critical threshold, because when the car is turning, the two wheels towards the center of the curve turn slower than the outer two. For this same reason, a differential is used in virtually all road-going vehicles.

If a fault develops in any part of the ABS, a warning light will usually be illuminated on the vehicle instrument panel, and the ABS will be disabled until the fault is rectified.

Additional Developments

Modern Electronic Stability Control (ESC) systems are an evolution of the ABS concept.

Here, a minimum of two additional sensors are added to help the system work: these are a steering wheel angle sensor, and a gyroscopic sensor. The theory of operation is simple: when the gyroscopic sensor detects that the direction taken by the car does not coincide with what the steering wheel sensor reports, the ESC software will brake the necessary individual wheel(s) (up to three with the most sophisticated systems), so that the vehicle goes the way the driver intends. The steering wheel sensor also helps in the operation of Cornering Brake Control (CBC), since this will tell the ABS that wheels on the inside of the curve should brake more than wheels on the outside, and by how much.

Traction Control

The ABS equipment may also be used to implement traction control system (TCS) on acceleration of the vehicle. If, when accelerating, the tire loses traction, the ABS controller can detect the situation and take suitable action so that traction is regained. Manufacturers often offer this as a separately priced option even though the infrastructure is largely shared with ABS. More sophisticated versions of this can also control throttle levels and brakes simultaneously.

Mercedes-Benz was the first to offer this electronic traction control system in 1985.

New Words

patent ['pætnt /'peitnt] n. 专利权, 专利品; 执照 v. 取得……的专利权, 请准专利
register ['redʒistə(r)] v. 登记, 申报, 注册
joint-venture n. 合资企业; 合营企业
technology [tek'nɔlədʒi] n. 技术, 科学技术
compose [kəm'pəuz] v. 组成, 作曲, 写作
rotational [rəu'teiʃnəl] adj. 转动的; 轮流的
condition [kən'diʃn] n. 情况; 环境; 状态; 形势
indicative [in'dikətiv] adj. 指示的, 表示……的, 象征的
pressure ['preʃə(r)] n. 压, 按, 榨 v. 对……施加压力; 迫使

via ['vaiə] prep. 经由, 通过, 经过
disregard [disri'gɑ:d] n. 忽视; 漠视 v. 不理会, 不顾
threshold ['θreʃhəuld] n. 门槛, 开端, 入口
curve [kə:v] n. 曲线, 曲球, 弯曲 v. 成曲形; 弯; 使弯曲
evolution [i:və'lu:ʃn] n. 进化, 进展, 发展
minimum ['minimǝm] n. 最小量 adj. 最小的; 最低的
coincide [kəuin'said] v. 一致; 符合
sophisticated [sə'fistikeitid] adj. 复杂的, 精密的
acceleration [æk,selə'reiʃn] n. 加速; 加速度
simultaneously [ˌsiməl'teiniəsli] adv. 同时地

Expressions

1. ABS (Anti-lock Brake System) 制动防抱死系统
2. CAB (Controller Anti-lock Brake) 防抱死制动控制器
3. ECU (Electronic Control Unit) 电控单元
4. wheel speed sensor 车轮转速传感器
5. ESC (Electronic Stability Control) 电子稳定控制系统
6. controller 控制器
7. valve 阀门
8. monitor 监视器
9. steering wheel angle sensor 方向盘角度传感器
10. gyroscopic sensor 陀螺仪传感器
11. CBC (Cornering Brake Control) 弯道制动控制
12. TCS (Traction Control System) 牵引力控制系统

Notes on the Text

1. A typical ABS is composed of a central electronic control unit (ECU), four wheel speed sensors—one for each wheel—and two or more hydraulic valves within the brake hydraulics
   一个典型的ABS是包括一个中央电子控制单元（ECU），4个轮速传感器——每个传感器负责一个轮子——和液压制动器中的两个或两个以上的液压阀。
   本句中间的one for each wheel为插入语。

2. The ECU is programmed to disregard differences in wheel rotative speed below a critical threshold, because when the car is turning, the two wheels towards the center of the curve turn slower than the outer two.
   ECU的设计使其无视车轮转速低于临界值时的差异，因为当汽车转弯时，朝着曲线中心的两个车轮比另外两个车轮转动慢。
   本句中because引导一个原因状语从句。

3. If a fault develops in any part of the ABS, a warning light will usually be illuminated on the vehicle instrument panel, and the ABS will be disabled until the fault is rectified.
   如果在ABS的任何部位发生故障，汽车仪表板上的警示灯通常会亮起，此时ABS将被禁用，直到故障排除。
   句中If引导一个条件状语从句。

Exercises

1. Fill in the blanks with the suitable terms according to the text.

| ABS | CAB | ECU | CBC | TCS | steering wheel angle sensor | gyroscopic sensor |
| monitor | wheel speed sensor | | controller | ESC | | |

(1) The anti-lock brake controller is also known as the _____.

(2) Modern _____ systems are an evolution of the ABS concept.

(3) Here, a minimum of two additional sensors are added to help the system work: these are a _____, and a _____.

(4) The steering wheel sensor also helps in the operation of _____, since this will tell the ABS that wheels on the inside of the curve should brake more than wheels on the outside, and by how much.

(5) The ABS equipment may also be used to implement _____ on acceleration of the vehicle.

(6) A typical ABS is composed of a central _____, four wheel speed sensors—one for each wheel — and two or more hydraulic valves within the brake hydraulics.

(7) When the _____ detects it is turning significantly faster than the others, brake hydraulic pressure to the wheel is increased so the braking force is reapplied and the wheel slows.

(8) If, when accelerating, the tire loses traction, the _____ controller can detect the situation and take suitable action so that traction is regained.

(9) The ECU constantly _____ the rotational speed of each wheel.

(10) When accelerating, the tire loses traction; the ABS _____ can detect the situation and take suitable action so that traction is regained.

2. Complete the following sentences with the words and phrases from the passage.

(1) The ECU constantly monitors the _____ of each wheel, and when it detects a wheel rotating significantly _____ than the others — a condition indicative of impending wheel lock — it _____ the valves to reduce hydraulic pressure to the brake at the affected wheel, thus _____ the braking force on that wheel.

(2) Here, a _____ of two additional sensors are added to help the system work: these are a _____, and a _____.

(3) The steering wheel sensor also helps in the _____ of Cornering Brake Control (CBC), since this will tell the ABS that wheels on the _____ of the curve should brake more than wheels on the _____, and by how much.

(4) Manufacturers often offer this as a _____ even though the infrastructure is largely shared with ABS.

3. Match the following English phrases in column A the Chinese equivalents in Column B.

A	B
ABS (Anti-lock Brake System)	控制器
CAB (Controller Anti-lock Brake)	车轮转速传感器
ECU (Electronic Control Unit)	陀螺仪传感器
CBC (Cornering Brake Control)	弯道制动控制
TCS (Traction Control System)	电控单元
ESC (Electronic Stability Control)	阀门
controller	电子稳定控制系统
steering wheel angle sensor	防抱死制动控制
gyroscopic sensor	牵引力控制系统
wheel speed sensor	方向盘角度传感器
valve	防抱死制动系统

4. Translate the following passages into Chinese.

(1) The ECU constantly monitors the rotational speed of each wheel, and when it detects a wheel rotating significantly slower than the others — a condition indicative of impending wheel lock — it actuates the valves to reduce hydraulic pressure to the brake at the affected wheel, thus reducing the braking force on that wheel.

(2) The theory of operation is simple: when the gyroscopic sensor detects that the direction taken by the car does not coincide with what the steering wheel sensor reports, the ESC software will brake the necessary individual wheel(s) (up to three with the most sophisticated systems), so that the vehicle goes the way the driver intends.

5. Training center practice:

(1) In a training center, in front of a real ABS, students are required to identify the main components and tell their corresponding English terms;

(2) Students are required to introduce the operation principle of an ABS by means of indicating the relating parts of it.

课文译文

制动系统

现代防抱死制动系统

在1975年，Bosch接管了一家叫做Teldix（Telefunken and Bendix的缩写）的欧洲公司，包括这家合资企业的注册专利，并且以此作为几年以后推入市场的新系统的基础。自上世纪70年代起，Bosch 和 Mercedes-Benz便开始合作，共同研发防抱死制动技术，并于1978年在卡车和梅赛德斯-奔驰S级汽车上引入了第一种完全的电子4轮多通道ABS系统。在更为现代的设计基础上推出的ABS系统，此后便广泛用于汽车和摩托车。

操作

这种防抱死制动控制器被称为CAB (Controller Anti-lock Brake)。

一个典型的ABS系统是由一个中心电控单元，四个车轮转速传感器组成——每个传感器用于一个车轮——和两个或者多个液压制动器当中的液压阀门组成。中心电控单元密切监视每个车轮的旋转速度，一旦它发现某个车轮的转速明显低于其他车轮——预示着这个车轮即将锁定——它就将启动阀门减少该车轮刹车的液压力，以此减少该车轮的制动力。车轮转动加快，当中心电控单元检测到车轮转动明显快于其他车轮时，该车轮制动液压力增加，制动力作用于车轮，由此车轮转速变慢。这样的过程不断重复，司机可以通过制动踏板的悸动察觉出来。一个典型的防抱死制动系统在一秒钟内增加和减少制动力的次数高达20次。

经设计，中心电控单元可以忽视低于临界值的车轮转动差异，因为汽车转弯时，朝向曲线中心的两个车轮比外侧两个转动要慢。由于这种原因，几乎所有的交通工具都使用了差异齿轮。

一旦ABS中任何一个部件出现故障，汽车仪表板上的警示灯就会亮起，ABS就会失灵，直到故障排除。

其他发展

电子稳定控制系统是ABS的发展。至少有两个额外的传感器被添加系统当中：一个是方向盘角度传感器，另一个是陀螺仪传感器。操作的原理很简单：当陀螺仪传感器检测到汽车没有按照方向盘角度传感器报告的方向行驶，ESC软件就会抑制相应的个别车轮，以此纠正汽车行驶的方向。方向盘角度传感器还对弯道制动控制有所帮助，因为它能告诉ABS转弯时内侧的车轮的制动应当强于外侧车轮，并且是强多少。

牵引力控制系统

ABS装置同样可以用来是在汽车加速时协助牵引力控制系统。如果在加速时，车轮失去牵引力，ABS控制器能够检测情况并采取适当措施恢复牵引。尽管该系统的基础构造很大部分是跟ABS共有的，但制造商通常是将其作为单独付费选项提供给用户。

1985年，梅赛德斯-奔驰首次使用电子牵引力控制系统。

Unit 9

Ignition System

Warming-up

1. Read the following passage independently with the questions provided below to think about.
   a. Which component is the most important part in an ignition system?
   b. How many different components of an ignition system are mentioned in the text?
   c. What is the function of the ignition coil?
   d. What is the function of the ignition module?
2. Write down the relevant terms and expressions in the space provided below.

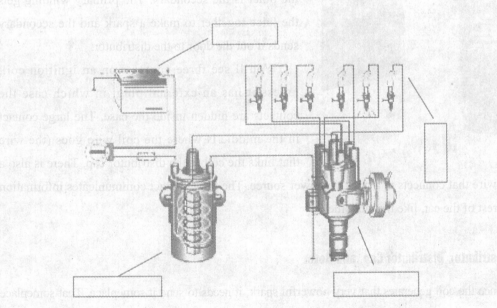

Text

Your engine is like a big pump. It pumps air and gas in, then pumps exhaust out. This ignition takes place thanks to a group of components working together, otherwise known as the ignition system. The ignition system consists of an ignition coil, distributor, distributor cap, rotor, plug wires and spark plugs. Older systems used a points-and-condenser system in the distributor, newer (as in most we'll ever see anymore) use an ECU, a little brain in a box, to control the spark and make slight changes in ignition timing. What do all of these components do?

The Ignition Coil

The ignition coil is the unit that takes your relatively weak battery power and turns it into a spark powerful enough to ignite fuel vapor. Inside a a traditional ignition coil are two coils of wire on top of each other. These coils are called windings. One winding is called the primary winding, the other is the secondary. The primary winding gets the juice together to make a spark and the secondary sends it out the door to the distributor.

You'll see three contacts on an ignition coil, unless it has an external plug, in which case the contacts are hidden inside the case. The large contact in the middle is where the coil wire goes (the wire that links the coil to the distributor cap. There is also a 12V+ wire that connects to a positive power source. The third contact communicates information to the rest of the car, like the tachometer.

The Distributor, Distributor Cap, and Rotor

Once the coil generates that very powerful spark, it needs to send it someplace. That someplace takes the spark and sends it out to the spark plugs, and that someplace is the distributor.

The distributor is basically a very precise spinner. As it spins, it distributes the sparks to the individual spark plugs at exactly the right time. It distributes the sparks by taking the powerful spark that came in via the coil wire and sending it through a spinning electrical contact known as the rotor. The rotor spins because it's connected directly to the shaft of the distributor. As the rotor spins, it makes contact with a number of points (4, 6, 8 or 12 depending on how many cylinders your engine has) and sends the spark through that point to the plug wire on the other end. Modern distributors have electronic assistance that can do things like alter the ignition timing.

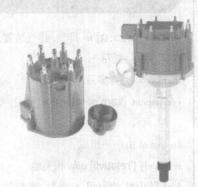

Spark Plugs and Wires

After the coil takes the weaker juice and makes a high powered spark, and the distributor takes the powerful spark and spins it to the right outlet, we need a way to take the spark to the spark plug. This is done through the spark plug wires. Each contact point on the distributor cap is connected to a plug wire that takes the spark to the spark plug.

The spark plugs are screwed into the cylinder head, which means that the end of the plug is sitting at the top of the cylinder where the action happen. At just the right time (thanks to the distributor), when the intake valves have let the right amount of fuel vapor and air into the cylinder, the spark plug makes a nice, blue, hot spark that ignites the mixture and creates combustion. At this point, the ignition system has done its job, a job it can do thousands of times per minute.

The Ignition Module

In the old days, a distributor relied on a lot of its own "mechanical intuition" to keep the spark timed perfectly. It did this through a setup called a points-and-condenser system. Ignition points were set to a specific gap that created optimum spark while the condenser regulated.

These days this is all handled by computers. The computer that directly regulates your ignition system is called the ignition module, or ignition control module. There is no maintenance or repair procedure for the module, other than replacement.

New Words

exhaust [ig'zɔːst] n. 排气, 排气装置, 废气 vt. 抽完, 用尽, 耗尽
thanks to 幸亏, 多亏, 由于
component [kəm'pəunənt] n. 成分, 组成部分, 部件, 元件
consist of 由……组成
relatively ['relətivli] adv. 相关地
fuel ['fjuːəl /'fjuəl] n. 燃料, 燃烧剂 v. 给……加燃料, 给……加油
vapor /'veipə US-ər/ n. 水汽, 水蒸气
traditional [trə'diʃnəl] adj. 传统的, 惯例的

precise [pri'sais] adj. 精确的, 准确的
individual [ˌindi'vidjuəl] adj. 个别的, 单独的
a number of 许多, 若干
electronic assistance 电子辅助
alter ['ɔːltə] v. 改变
be screwed into 被拧入
happen ['hæpən] v. 发生; 偶然; 碰巧
the amount of 数量，数额
rely on 依赖, 依靠
optimum ['ɔptiməm] n. 最适宜 adj. 最适宜的
replacement [ri'pleismənt] n. 交换, 代替者, 更换

Expressions

1. engine n. 引擎, 提供动力的机器
2. ignition system 点火系统，点火装置
3. pump n. 泵 v. 泵
4. ignition coil 点火线圈, 发火线圈
5. distributor 分电器
6. distributor cap 分电器盖
7. rotor n. 转子, 转动体, 回转轴
8. ignition module 点火控制器
9. plug wire n. 高压线
10. spark plug 火花塞
11. points-and-condenser 触点和电容
12. ECU (electronic control unit) 电子控制单元
13. valve n. 活瓣, 活门, 阀
14. winding n. 线圈, 绕组
15. tachometer n. 转速计, 流速计
16. spinner n. 旋转器 (整流罩, 快速回转工具)
17. shaft n. 轴, 杆状物
18. cylinder head 气缸盖

Notes on the Text

1. The ignition system consists of an ignition coil, distributor, distributor cap, rotor, plug wires and spark plugs.
   点火系包括点火线圈、分电器、分电器盖、转子、插线和火星塞。
   句中consist of 意为:"包含,包括,由……组成"。

2. The ignition coil is the unit that takes your relatively weak battery power and turns it into a spark powerful enough to ignite fuel vapor.
   点火线圈是一个元件,它将相对较弱的电池电量转变为足够强的火花,用于点燃燃油气。
   句中that引导一个表语从句,该从句中and连接两个并列成分。句中enough修饰形容词后置。

3. It distributes the sparks by taking the powerful spark that came in via the coil wire and sending it through a spinning electrical contact known as the rotor.
   分电器分配火花是先将通过线圈进入的火花吸收,再将它通过一个旋转的点接触,也就是我们常说的转子分配出去。
   句中by后面跟两个宾语,分别为taking和sending,他们又是由and并列起来。known as的意思是:"通常所说的"。

4. Ignition points were set to a specific gap that created optimum spark while the condenser regulated.
   点火点被设置为一个特殊的间隙,它能进行最适宜的点火而冷却剂又得到了控制。
   本句中were set to是被动语态,created是过去时表主动,regulated 是过去分词表示被动。

5. The computer that directly regulates your ignition system is called the ignition module, or ignition control module.
   直接控制你的点火系的电脑被称为点火控制器。
   句中that引导一个定语从句。

Exercises

1. Fill in the blanks with the suitable terms according to the text.

ignition system	distributor	cylinder head	ignition coil	spinner
distributor cap	ignition module	spark plug	winding	rotor

1. This ignition takes place thanks to a group of components working together, otherwise known as the _____.

2. The distributor is basically a very precise _____.

3. The computer that directly regulates your ignition system is called the _____, or ignition control module.

4. The large contact in the middle is where the coil wire goes (the wire that links the coil to the _____.

5. The spark plugs are screwed into the _____, which means that the end of the plug is sitting at the top of the cylinder where the action happen.

6. The primary winding gets the juice together to make a spark and the secondary sends it out the door to the _____.

7. The _____ is the unit that takes your relatively weak battery power and turns it into a spark powerful enough to ignite fuel vapor.

8. It distributes the sparks by taking the powerful spark that came in via the coil wire and sending it through a spinning electrical contact known as the _____.

9. The primary _____ gets the juice together to make a spark and the secondary sends it out the door to the distributor.

10. The _____ are screwed into the cylinder head, which means that the end of the plug is sitting at the top of the cylinder where the action happens.

2. Complete the following sentences with the words and phrases from the passage.

(1) Your _____ is like a big pump. It _____ air and gas in, then pumps exhaust out.

(2) Older systems used a _____ system in the distributor, newer (as in most we'll ever see anymore) use an _____, a little brain in a box, to control the spark and make slight _____ in _____.

(3) At just the _____ (thanks to the distributor), when the _____ have let the right amount of _____ and air into the _____, the spark plug makes a nice, blue, hot spark that ignites the _____ and creates _____.

(4) In the old days, a _____ relied on a lot of its own "mechanical intuition" to keep the spark timed perfectly.

(5) The computer that directly _____ your ignition system is called the _____, or _____ ignition control module.

3. Match the following English phrases in column A the Chinese equivalents in Column B.

A	B
ignition system	分电器
ignition coil	转子, 转动体, 回转轴
istributor cap	旋转器(整流罩,快速回转工具)

distributor	点火线圈,发火线圈
rotor	火花塞
ignition module	活动和固定触点
spark plug	线圈,绕组
points-and-condenser	点火系统，点火装置
winding	气缸盖
cylinder head	转速计,流速计
spinner	点火控制器
tachometer	分电器盖

4. Translate the following passages into Chinese.

(1) This ignition takes place thanks to a group of components working together, otherwise known as the ignition system. The ignition system consists of an ignition coil, distributor, distributor cap, rotor, plug wires and spark plugs.

_____

_____

(2) One winding is called the primary winding, the other is the secondary. The primary winding gets the juice together to make a spark and the secondary sends it out the door to the distributor.

_____

_____

5. Training center practice:

(1) In a training center, in front of a real ignition system, students are required to identify the main components and tell their corresponding English terms;

(2) Students are required to introduce the operation principle of an ignition system by means of indicating the relating parts of it.

Learn and Write

Applied Writing:　Notice

通知的写法

　　通知是上级对下级、组织对成员或平行单位之间部署工作、传达事情或召开会议等所使用的应用文。通知的写法有两种，一种是以布告形式贴出，把事情通知有关人员，如学生、观众等，通常不用称呼；另一种是口头通知的形式，通知有关人员，此种通知形式要求言简意赅、措辞得当、时间及时。

　　1. 布告形式的通知：通常此类通知上方正中写Notice或NOTICE（通知），发出通知

单位的具体名称可放在正文前,也可放在正文后,发出通知的日期写在右上角处。例如:

NOTICE

May 14, 2000

　　All professors and associate professors are requested to meet in the college conference room on Saturday, August 18, at 2:00 p. m. to discuss questions of international academic exchanges.

---

　　2. 口头通知用词表达要注重口语化。口头通知的开头往往有称呼语(被通知的对象),如:"Boys and girls","Ladies and gentlemen","Comrades and friends"等,或用提醒听众注意的语句,如"Attention,please!""Your attention,please!""May I have your attention, please?"等,且最好有结束语,如:"Thank you(for listening)"以示礼貌。

课 文 译 文

发动机点火和起动系统

　　发动机就像是一个大的泵。它吸入空气和可燃气体,然后排出废气。点火依靠一组零部件共同工作完成的,也就是所谓的点火系。点火系包括点火线圈、分电器、分电器盖、转子、插线和火花塞。旧的点火系在分电器当中使用的是活动和固定触点装置,而新型的(正如在大多数时候我们看到的)是使用ECU,像一个装在盒子里的大脑,以控制火花,并对点火正时进行细微的改变。这些零部件是做什么的呢?

点火线圈

　　点火线圈是一个元件,它将相对较弱的电池电量转变为足够强的高压电,用于点燃可燃混合气。在传统的点火线圈当中,有两个线圈分别装在两个顶部。这两个线圈被称为绕组,一个是初级绕组,另外一个是次级绕组,初级绕组聚合电流产生火花的能量,次级绕组将高压电送到分电器。

　　您会看到点火线圈有三个接线柱,除非它有一个外部的插件,而在这种情况下,接线柱是隐藏在其中的。中间部分大的接线柱就是线圈线出口的地方(它将线圈和分电器盖的顶端连接起来),12V+的线连接电流的正极。第三个接线柱传送汽车的其他信息,比如转速表。

分电器，分电器盖和转子

一旦线圈产生的非常强大的高压电，就需要把它送到某个地方。所谓的某个地方要能接收火花并将其传送到火花塞，而所谓的某个地方就是分电器。分电器本质上讲是一个非常精确的旋转器，当它旋转的时候，它将高压电以准确的时间发送到个别的火花塞。分电器分配高压电是先将通过线圈进入的高压电引入，再将它通过一个旋转的点接触，也就是我们常说的转子分配出去。转子旋转是因为它直接连接到分电器的轴，当转子旋转时，它跟大量的点产生接触（4个，6个，8个或者12个，这取决于你的引擎有多少汽缸），并通过这些接触点将高压电转送另一端的插线。

火花塞和插线

在线圈利用电磁感应产生高压电后，分电器通过旋转将高压电分配到适合的出口，这时我们就需要一种途径将高压电送到火花塞。这种途径就是火花塞高压线。分电器帽上的每一个接触点都相同的高压线相连，用以将高压电传送到火花塞。

火花塞是拧入缸盖的，这就意味着火花塞的末端就放置在汽缸的顶部。在适当的时候（这取决于分电器），也就是当进气门将适当数量的燃油蒸汽和空气吸入汽缸，火花塞就产生一个美丽的蓝色火花点燃可燃混合气并进行燃烧。至此，点火系就完成了它的工作，这种工作每分钟可以完成数千次。

点火控制器

在过去，分电器是依靠自身的"直觉"来确定火花的准确时间。它通过一个叫做触点和电容的装置完成上述工作。通过调整触点设置一个特定的间隙，以产生最佳的火花。

现在，这一切都由电脑来完成。直接控制你的点火系的电脑被称为点火控制器。它除了更换以外，没有其他的维护和修理的办法。

Unit 10

Battery, Lights and Signal System

Warming-up

1. Read the following passage independently with the questions provided below to think about.
   a. What's the purpose of the battery?
   b. How many kinds of battery can you name out?
   c. What are the functions of the charging system?
   d. How many parts are included in the lighting system in a typical automobile?
2. Write down the relevant terms and expressions in the space provided below.

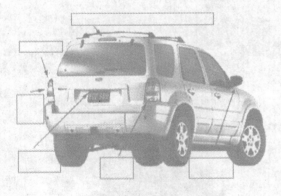

Text

The purpose of the battery is to store electrical energy. It does this by converting the electrical energy supplied to it into chemical energy so that when an electrical current is required the energy change is reversed.

In making the battery, several similar plates are properly spaced and welded to form a plate group. Plates of two types are used, one for the positive plate group, the other for the negative plate group. A positive plate is nested with a negative plate group, with separators placed between the plates to form an element. Separators are designed to hold the plates apart so that they do not touch, and at the same time they must be porous enough to permit electrolyte to circulate between the plates.

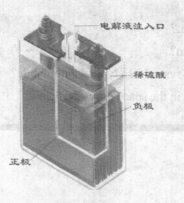

Lead-acid Battery

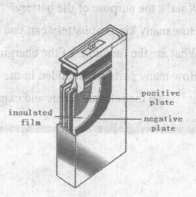

Nickel-hydrogen Battery

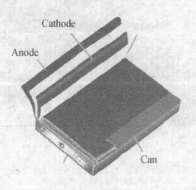

Lithium-ion Battery

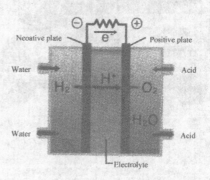

Hydrogen Fuel Cell

The charging system provides the electrical energy a car needs once its engine starts. The charging system does two jobs. First, it provides electrical power for the ignition system and the car's electrical accessories. Second, it replaces the power used by the battery in starting the car. In other words, the charging system maintains the battery's state of charge.

Let us imagine that the wire loop is rotated between the north and south poles of the magnetic field. If the ends of the loop are now connected via collector rings and carbon brushes to a voltmeter, it will be possible to read off an alternating voltage owing to the constantly changing position of the loop with respect to the poles.

Electricity can be produced by moving a conductor through a magnetic field. The opposite also holds true. By moving the magnetic field and holding the conductor, electricity can be generated in the conductor. This current is called an induced current. This is the basic principle of the alternator, an electromechanical device that changes mechanical energy into electrical energy.

Electric motors (DC, AC and three-phase), as well as hydraulic and pneumatic motors are used as starting motors for internal-combustion engines.

The lighting system in a typical automobile includes the headlights, direction-signal lights, side marker lights, brake lights, tail lights, and the interior lights. The interior lights include instrument-panel lights, various warning, indicator, and courtesy lights which turn on when a car door is opened.

Plastics are rapidly updating car lighting systems. Glass headlight lenses have been virtually replaced by transparent polycarbonate plastics. These plastics are designed to resist high levels of heat, are shatter-resistant, and can be molded into almost any shape. This gives car designers and engineers far more flexibility in the styling and placement of headlights. Plastics' versatility also allows auto headlights to incorporate high-tech focusing designs in the lenses, providing the benefit of increased highway safety.

Tail lights, turn signals, cornering lamps, back-up lights, and fog lights are all made of polycarbonate plastics or, in some cases, acrylic plastics. These lenses have similar design and engineering advantages to auto headlight lenses, and incorporate reflective optical surfaces too.

Major changes in the future of both head and tail light systems are imminent, with the incorporation of plastic-based LED (Light Emitting Diode) brake-light systems and "light box" systems, whereby an easily accessible, single light source is used to provide exterior lighting for the car via acrylic fiber-optic wires. The incorporation of "light box" LED car lighting technology will eliminate the need for high-heat resistant plastics in auto lighting systems, allowing substitution for even lighter plastic lenses that retain the ability to resist impacts.

New Words

battery ['bætəri] n. 电池
current ['kʌrənt] n. 电流, 水流, 气流
weld [weld] v. 焊接 n. 焊接, 焊缝
element ['elimənt] n. 要素, 元素, 成分, 元件, 自然环境
electrolyte [i'lektrəʊlait] n. 电解, 电解液
cathode ['kæθəud] n. 阴极
anode ['ænəud] n. [电]阳极, 正极
accessory [æk'sesəri] n. 附件, 零件, 附加物 adj. 附属的, 补充的, 副的
magnetic [mæg'netik] adj. 磁的, 有磁性的, 有吸引力的
voltmeter ['vəʊlt,mi:tə(r)] n. 伏特计, 电压表
pneumatic [nju(:)'mætik] adj. 汽力的, 气动的

Expressions

1. positive plate 阳[正]极板
2. negative plate 负[阴]极板
3. lead-acid Battery 铅酸电池
4. nickel-hydrogen Battery 镍氢电池
5. lithium-ion Battery 锂离子电池
6. hydrogen Fuel Cell 氢燃料电池
7. alternating voltage 交流电压
8. induced current 感生电流

Notes on the Text

1. It does this by converting the electrical energy supplied to it into chemical energy so that when an electrical current is required the energy change is reversed.
   It 在句子中代指battery，so that 带一个从句表示"以便，以至"。is reversed 表"相反"。
   蓄电池将电能转变为化学能储存，在用电时再将化学能转变为电能。

2. If the ends of the loop are now connected via collector rings and carbon brushes to a voltmeter, it will be possible to read off an alternating voltage owing to the constantly changing position of the loop with respect to the poles.
   如果线圈的一端通过集电环和电刷与伏特计相连，将能够读取由于线圈相对于磁极不停的改变位置而产生的交流电压。

BATTERY, LIGHTS AND SIGNAL SYSTEM UNIT 10 91

via 是介词，"经过，通过"。一般用via...to... "经过某物与某物"。

owing to "由于，因某缘故"

with respect to "相对于"

3. Electricity can be produced by moving a conductor through a magnetic field. The opposite also holds true.

导体在磁场中移动会产生电流，反之也成立。opposite 表相反。

4. Electric motors (DC, AC and three-phase), as well as hydraulic and pneumatic motors are used as starting motors for internal-combustion engines.

DC的意思是"直流电"，AC"交流电"，three-phase "三相交流电"。

as well as "和……一样，和……一起"。

be used as "被用作"。

直流电机、交流电机和三相交流电机，以及液压和气压电机都可用作内燃机的起动机。

Exercises

1. Fill in the blanks with the suitable terms according to the text.

| electrolyte | accessory | hydraulic | pneumatic | alternating |
| voltage | induced current | | charging system | separators |

(1) Electric motors, as well as _____ and _____ motors are used as starting motors for internal-combustion engines.

(2) By moving the magnetic field and holding the conductor, electricity can be generated in the conductor. This current is called an _____.

(3) One of the _____'s jobs is providing electrical power for the ignition system and the car's electrical _____.

(4) _____ are designed to hold the plates apart so that they do not touch, and at the same time they must be porous enough to permit _____ to circulate between the plates.

(5) It will be possible to read off an _____ owing to the constantly changing position of the loop with respect to the poles.

2. Complete the following sentences with the words and phrases from the passage.

(1) The purpose of the _____ is to store electrical energy. It does this by converting the electrical energy supplied to it into _____ so that when an _____ is required the energy change is reversed.

(2) Plates of two types are used, one for the _____, the other for the _____.

(3) Electricity can be produced by moving a conductor through a _____. The opposite also holds true.

(4) This is the basic principle of the alternator, an electromechanical device that changes _____ into _____.

(5) The interior lights include _____ lights, various warning, indicator, and _____ lights which turn on when a car door is opened.

3. **Match the following English phrases in column A the Chinese equivalents in Column B.**

A	B
element	转向信号灯
magnetic	尾灯
direction-signal lights	元素
brake lights	门控灯
tail lights	磁性的
interior lights	刹车灯
courtesy lights	车内灯

4. **Translate the following passages into Chinese.**

(1) The charging system does two jobs. First, it provides electrical power for the ignition system and the car's electrical accessories. Second, it replaces the power used by the battery in starting the car. In other words, the charging system maintains the battery's state of charge.

(2) A positive plate is nested with a negative plate group, with separators placed between the plates to form an element. Separators are designed to hold the plates apart so that they do not touch, and at the same time they must be porous enough to permit electrolyte to circulate between the plates.

5. **Training center practice:**

(1) In a training center, in front of a real battery, students are required to identify the main components and tell their corresponding English terms;

(2) Students are required to introduce the name of each light in the lighting system of an automobile in English.

课文译文

电源及照明系统

蓄电池用于储存电能,它将电能转变为化学能储存,在用电时再将化学能转变为电能。

在制造蓄电池时,几块相似的极板以适当的间隔焊在一起组成极板组。极板组分为两种,阳极板组和阴极板组。一块阳极板被一组阴极板所包围,隔板放在两组极板之间形成一个单元。隔板又必须具有多孔性,使电解液能够在各极板间流动。

一旦开始发动,充电系统就给汽车提供电能。充电系统有两个任务:首先,给点火系和电力附件提供电能;其次,给电池补充在起步时消耗的电能,换句话说,就是维持电池的电荷状态。

假设线圈在磁场中的南极和北极间转动。如果线圈的一端通过集电环和电刷与伏特计相连,将能够读取由于线圈相对于磁极不停的改变位置而产生的交流电压。

导体在磁场中移动会产生电流,反之也成立。保持导体固定不动,移动磁场,导体中就会产生电流,该电流称为感应电流。发电机的基本原理就是这样的,通过机电装置把机械能转变为电能。

直流电机、交流电机和三相交流电机,以及液压和气压电机都可用作内燃机的起动机。

标准汽车照明系统包括前灯、转向信号灯、侧灯、停车灯、刹车灯、尾灯和车内灯。车内灯包括仪表板灯、各种警告灯、指示灯和车门打开时自动开启的门控灯。

塑料正在迅速更新汽车照明系统。大灯玻璃镜片实际上已被透明的聚碳酸酯塑料取代。这些塑料能抵抗高温,防碎,几乎可以被铸造成任何形状。这就使得汽车设计师和工程师在造型和大灯安置方面有了更强的灵活性。塑料的多功能性也让汽车头灯在镜片设计方面融入了更多高科技的含量,也为增强公路安全提供了帮助。

尾灯、转向灯、转弯灯、倒车灯和雾灯都是由聚碳酸酯塑料制成,或在某些情况下,用有机玻璃制造。这些镜头有着与汽车大灯镜类似的设计和技术优势,同时具有表面反光的特点。

对于汽车头灯和尾灯的重大改变以迫在眉睫,随着以塑料为基础的LED(发光二极管)刹车灯系统和灯箱的系统的融合,一个便利的、单光源的照明系统可通过丙烯酸光纤线为汽车提供外部照明。这种技术使得汽车照明不再需要抗高热塑料,取而代之的是更明亮且同样抗压的新型塑料透镜。

Unit 11 Car Maintenance (I)

Warming-up

1. Read the following passage independently with the questions provided below to think about.
   a. What does car maintenance mean?
   b. Why do we need car maintenance?
   c. Does the actual schedule of car maintenance vary depending on the Make of a car?
   d. Can you list some common car maintenance tasks(at least 3)?
2. Write down the relevant terms and expressions below.

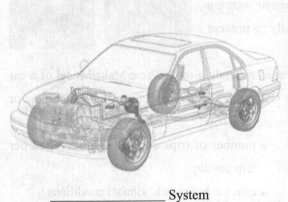

_____ System

Picture 1

_____

Picture 2

Text

Car maintenance means to inspect or test the condition of car subsystems (e.g., engine) and service or replace parts which become out of order or broken (known as repair or unscheduled maintenance) as well as perform the routine actions which keep the device in working order (known as scheduled maintenance) or prevent trouble from arising (preventive maintenance). Unscheduled maintenance is conducted to get equipment working again. Scheduled and preventive maintenance is conducted to keep equipment working and/or extend the life of the equipment.

The primary goal of maintenance is to avoid or mitigate the consequences of failure of equipment. It is designed to preserve and restore equipment reliability by replacing worn components before they actually fail, by preventing the failure before it actually occurs. Regular maintenance is critical to ensure the safety, reliability, drivability, comfort and longevity of a car. A number of parts are replaced preventively to avoid major damage or even safety issues, e.g. timing belt replacement.

Maintenance, including routinely washing and waxing your car, going through a full annual inspection, making seasonal preparations, knowing what engine repair warning signs to recognize, and performing specifically to prevent faults from occurring.

The actual schedule of car maintenance varies depending on the Year/Make/Model of a car and its driving conditions and driver behavior. Car makers recommend the so-called extreme or the ideal service schedule based on impact parameters such as

- number of trips and distance travelled per trip per day
- extreme hot or cold climate conditions
- mountainous, dusty or iced roads
- heavy stop and go vs. long distance cruising
- towing a trailer and other heavy load

Experienced service advisors in dealerships

Auto Body Collision Repair System

and independent shops recommend schedule intervals, which are often in-between the ideal or extreme service schedule. They base it on the driving conditions and behavior of the car owner/driver.

Common car maintenance tasks include:
- car wash
- check or flush the engine oil and replace fuel filters
- inspect or replace windshield wipers
- check or refill windshield washer fluid
- inspect tires for pressure and wear
- tire balancing
- tire rotation
- wheel alignment
- check, clean or replace battery terminals and top up battery fluid
- inspect or replace brake pads
- check or flush brake fluid

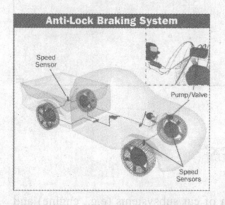

- check or flush transmission fluid
- check or flush power steering fluid
- check and flush engine coolant
- inspect or replace spark plugs
- inspect or replace air filter
- inspect or replace timing belt and other belts
- lubricate locks, latches, hinges
- check all lights
- tighten chassis nuts / bolts
- check if rubber boots are cracked and need replacement
- test electronics, e.g., Anti-lock braking system or ABS

Some tasks that have equivalent service intervals are combined into one single service known as a tune up. Modern cars, where electronics control most of the car's functions, the traditional tune up doesn't apply anymore. Maintenance jobs like a tune up used to mean getting the engine's performance back on track. Today embedded software takes care of it by checking constantly thousands of sensor signals compensating for worn out spark plugs, clogged filters, etc. The so-called limp-home function lets you drive on limited power when your engine is in trouble. In the old days this might have meant a break down.

In some countries, the completed services are recorded in a service book which is rubber stamped by the service centre upon completion of each service. A complete service history usually adds to the resale value of a vehicle.

New Words

maintenance ['meintinəns] *n.* 维修，保养
inspect [in'spekt] *v.* 检查，视察
unscheduled [ʌn'ʃedju:ld] *adj.* 不定期的(没有预定时间的)
scheduled ['ʃedju:ld] *adj.* 预定的
preventive [pri'ventiv] *adj.* 预防的

parameter [pə'ræmitə] *n.* 参数,参量
interval ['intəvəl] *n.* 间隔，间距
latch [lætʃ] *n.* 挂钩,止动销
hinge [hindʒ] *n.* 铰链
stamp [stæmp] *v.* 印上印记，盖章 *n.* 印；标志，印记

Expressions

1. car wash 汽车清洗
2. wheel alignment 车轮定位
3. tune up 校准
4. clogged filter 阻塞的滤清器
5. anti-lock braking system (ABS)防抱死系统

Notes on the Text

1. Car maintenance means to inspect or test the condition of car subsystems (e.g., engine) and service or replace parts which become out of order or broken (known as repair or unscheduled maintenance) as well as perform the routine actions which keep the device in working order (known as scheduled maintenance) or prevent trouble from arising (preventive maintenance).

   汽车保养意味着要检查或测试汽车子系统（例如，发动机）的状况和保养或是更换工作不正常或损坏的部件（也叫修理或不定期维修），以及进行定期检查使设备保持正常（也叫定期维修）或是预防问题升级（预防性维修）。

   句中to inspect，perform，prevent为不定式并列成分。

2. Maintenance, including routinely washing and waxing your car, going through a full annual inspection, making seasonal preparations, knowing what engine repair warning signs to recognize, and performing specifically to prevent faults from occurring.

   维修，包括定期性地给车清洗、上蜡，完整的年检，季节性的检查，知道发动机修理警告信号，以及具体操作来预防故障发生。

本句中including引导伴随状语，其中washing and waxing, going through, making, knowing, performing作并列成分。

3. In some countries, the completed services are recorded in a service book which is rubber stamped by the service centre upon completion of each service.
在一些国家，完整的维护在每次完成后都要记录在服务手册上并盖章。完整的维护记录通常可以增加转卖汽车的价值。
which 引导定语从句，先行词为service book。

Exercises

1. Fill in the blanks with the suitable terms according to the text.

| unscheduled | Model | preventively | sensor | performance |
| service centre | limp-home | preventive | maintenance | tune up |

(1) _____ maintenance is conducted to get equipment working again.

(2) Scheduled and _____ maintenance is conducted to keep equipment working and/or extend the life of the equipment.

(3) The primary goal of _____ is to avoid or mitigate the consequences of failure of equipment.

(4) A number of parts are replaced _____ to avoid major damage or even safety issues, e.g. timing belt replacement.

(5) The actual schedule of car maintenance varies depending on the Year/Make/_____ of a car and its driving conditions and driver behavior.

(6) Some tasks that have equivalent service intervals are combined into one single service known as a _____.

(7) Maintenance jobs like a tune up used to mean getting the engine's _____ back on track.

(8) Today embedded software takes care of it by checking constantly thousands of signals compensating for worn out spark plugs, clogged filters, etc.

(9) The so-called _____ function lets you drive on limited power when your engine is in trouble. In the old days this might have meant a break down.

(10) In some countries, the completed services are recorded in a service book which is rubber stamped by the _____ upon completion of each service. A complete service history usually adds to the resale value of a vehicle.

2. Complete the following sentences with the words and phrases from the passage.

(1) Car _____ to inspect or test the condition of car _____s (e.g., engine) and service or replace parts which become out of order or broken (known as repair or unscheduled maintenance) as well as perform the routine actions which keep the device in working order (known as _____ maintenance) or prevent trouble from arising (_____ maintenance).

(2) It is designed to preserve and restore equipment reliability by replacing _____ components before they actually fail, by preventing the failure before it actually occurs. _____ maintenance is critical to ensure the safety, reliability, drivability, comfort and longevity of a car.

(3) Maintenance, including _____ washing and waxing your car, going through a full _____ _____, making seasonal preparations, knowing what engine repair warning signs to recognize, and performing specifically to prevent _____ from occurring.

3. Match the following English phrases in column A the Chinese equivalents in Column B.

A	B
maintenance	定期检查
parameter	汽车清洗
car wash	校准
tune up	防抱死系统
Anti-lock braking system	参数
scheduled inspect	维修，保养排气冲程

4. Translate the following passages into Chinese.

(1) Some tasks that have equivalent service intervals are combined into one single service known as a tune up.

(2) Unscheduled maintenance is conducted to get equipment working again.

(3) Scheduled and preventive maintenance is conducted to keep equipment working and/or extend the life of the equipment.

(4) The primary goal of maintenance is to avoid or mitigate the consequences of failure of equipment.

(5) A complete service history usually adds to the resale value of a vehicle.

5. Training center practice:

1) In a training center, students are required to give regular maintenance for certain cars;
2) Students are required to name each step in an regular maintenance for certain cars.

Learn and Write

Applied Writing: Application

申请表

申请表的表格填写较为简单，语言简单明了，格式有类似之处，但还是要仔细阅读其要求（instruction），按照要求填写。

填写表格要求书写清楚，如有些表格中上常有Please Print或Please Write in Block Capitals的字样。Print的意思是用印刷体书写，而不用手写体，每个字母都分开写。Write in Block Capitals意思是印刷体大写字母。签名(Signature)应该用手写体。

Office Use Only（仅供办公室用）或Bank Use Only（仅供银行用）等部分不必填写。

Nationality或Citizenship指国籍，应使用国名的形容词形式，如Chinese, Japanese, British。其他常用表达：

1. GENDER（性别）
2. CORRESPONDENCE ADDRESS（通信地址）
3. COUNTRY OF PERMANENT RESIDENCE（永久留居国）
4. SALARY EXPECTED（预期薪水）
5. MARITAL STATUS（婚姻状况）
6. OCCUPATION（职业）
7. NATIONALITY AT BIRTH（出生国籍）
8. PROPOSED DURATION OF STAY（逗留时间）
9. TITLE（头衔）
10. FULL NAME（全名）

Sample:

```
Application
Surname/family name_____  Title: Mr./Mrs./Miss/Ms.(Please circle)
Other name/s _____
Date of birth(dd/mm/yy)_____/_____/_____  Gender_____
Marital status_____
Nationality_____  Nationality of Birth_____
Permanent address_____
Correspondence address_____
Occupation_____
Telephone_____   Fax_____   E-mail_____
```

课 文 译 文

汽车维修（Ⅰ）

　　汽车维修意味着要检查或测试汽车子系统（例如，发动机）的状况，保养或是更换工作不正常或损坏的部件（也叫修理或不定期维修），以及进行定期检查使设备保持正常（也叫定期维修）或是预防问题升级（预防性维修）。不定期维修是使设备再次工作。定期和预防性维修是使设备持续工作或是延长设备工作期。

　　维修的基本目标是防止或减轻设备故障。它被定义为通过在受损部件完全失效前更换它们，或是故障产生之前预防。定期维修对于确保汽车安全性、可靠性、驾驶性能、舒适度和寿命非常关键。一些部件预防性地更换是为了避免重大损坏甚至是安全问题，如正时齿带的更换。

　　维修，包括定期性地给车清洗、上蜡，完整的年检，季节性的检查，知道发动机修理警告信号，以及具体操作来预防故障发生。

　　汽车维修的实际安排根据汽车年限、生产、型号以及它的驾驶环境和驾驶员反应的不同有所不同。汽车生产商建议那种所谓的极度的或是理想化的维护是基于以下的影响参数：

- 每天出行的次数和每次出行的远近距离
- 极热或极冷的天气状况
- 山区坡地、多尘的或是结冰的路面
- 强行停车和启动或是长距离出游
- 牵引拖车或和其他的重负载

　　汽车代理和自主经销商店里经验丰富的保养顾问建议定期保养，这通常是相对于理想化的或极度保养的折中。基于驾驶环境和驾驶员的反应。

　　通常汽车保养任务包括：

- 汽车清洗
- 检查或补足汽车发动机机油以及更换燃油滤清器
- 检查或更换挡风玻璃雨刮器
- 检查或重新加满挡风玻璃清洗液
- 检查轮胎压力和磨损
- 轮胎平衡
- 轮胎旋转
- 车轮定位
- 检查、补足或更换电池终端并装满电池液

- 检查或更换制动片
- 检查或补足制动液
- 检查或补足变速器液
- 检查或补足动力转向液
- 检查或补足冷却液
- 检查或更换火花塞
- 检查或更换空气滤清器
- 检查或更换正时齿带或其它皮带
- 润滑锁、挂钩和铰链
- 检查所有照明
- 紧固底盘螺母、螺栓
- 检查橡胶垫片是否开裂是否需要更换
- 检查电气设备，如防抱死系统

一些有相等的间隔时间的维护结合在一起合成一种服务，称作调校。电气系统控制汽车大部分功能的现代汽车中不再使用传统的调校。像调校一类的维护工作过去意味着让发动机性能回到正轨。现在嵌入式软件通过经常检查成千的传感器信号来修正磨损的火花塞、阻塞了的滤清器等等。所谓的"跛行回家"功能让你当发动机出问题时能用仅有的能量驾驶。过去这可能就意味着抛锚。

在一些国家，完整的维护在每次完成后都要记录在服务手册上并盖章。完整的维护记录通常可以增加转卖汽车的价值。

Unit 12

Car Maintenance (II)

Warming-up

1. Read the following passage independently with the questions provided below to think about.
   a. What is OTC?
   b. What is Auto Wheel Alignment?
   c. What are the functions of Wheel Alignment?
   d. What is oscillograph used for?
2. Write down the relevant terms and expressions below.

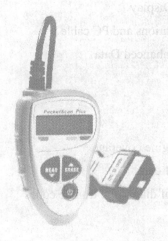

Auto _____ Tool

Picture 1

Picture 2

Text

Due to the increasingly complicated nature of the technology that is now incorporated into automobiles, most automobile dealerships now provide sophisticated diagnostic computers and various instruments to each technician, without which they would be unable to diagnose or repair a vehicle. They are various in types and brands. For instance, OTC, which is famous for its scan tools, is a major manufacturer and supplier of vehicle electronic diagnostic instruments, automotive fuel system maintenance equipment, special service tools, and general purpose tools, etc.

The following is a rough guide to some of the major tools for maintenance.

Auto Scan Tools

Because they are easy to use, Auto Scan Tools are widely used in auto maintenance. Here are some samples:

The USA 2007 Domestic Scan Kit now with brilliant color display, includes Body and Chassis system coverage to go along with Engine, Transmission, ABS, and Airbag. Other new features include: Repair Information, etc.

USA 2007 Domestic Scan Kit

Features:

- NEW-Brilliant Color Display
- NEW-USB communications and PC cable
- Domestic and Asian Enhanced Data
- No adapters to buy
- Data Graphing
- Record / Playback
- Gasoline and diesel engine coverage
- Automatic recording of data
- On-screen definitions of diagnostic trouble codes
- Internet upgradeable

 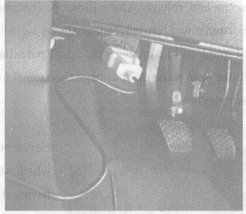

Plug your scan tool into the standard connector under the driver's side dashboard. Turn the key and let the tool initialize, keying in any data it asks for, such as the make, model and engine type. Now you can read trouble codes, erase them, check to see if any readiness monitors aren't complete.

Auto Wheel Alignment

A wheel alignment is part of standard automobile maintenance that consists of adjusting the angles of the wheels so that they are set to the car maker's specification.

Reduced Tire Wear

The purpose of these adjustments is maximum tire life. Improper alignment is a major cause of premature tire wear, while properly aligned vehicle can add thousands of miles to tire life.

Better Fuel Mileage

Fuel mileage increases as rolling resistance decreases. Total alignment sets all four wheel parallel which minimizes rolling resistance.

Adjusting wheel alignment

Improved Handling

Many handling problems can be corrected by total alignment. With all the system components aligned properly, road shock is more efficiently absorbed for a smoother ride.

Safer Driving

A suspension system inspection is part of alignment procedure. This allows us to spot worn parts before they cause problems.

Oscillograph

An oscillograph is an instrument for measuring alternating or varying electric current in terms of current and voltage. An oscilloscope (commonly abbreviated to scope or O-scope) is a type of electronic test instrument that allows signal voltages to be viewed, usually as a two-dimensional graph of one or more electrical potential differences (vertical axis) plotted as a function of time or of some other voltage (horizontal axis). There are two instruments that are in common use today:

- Electromagnetic oscillograph: An electromagnetic oscillograph is an Oscillograph which measures variations of electric current by having it go through a magnetic coil. Variations in current induce momentum in the coil, which can be directly measured.

- Cathode-ray oscilloscope: Originally all oscilloscopes used cathode-ray tubes as their display element and linear amplifiers for signal processing, but modern oscilloscopes can have LCD or LED screens, high-speed analog-to-digital converters and digital signal processors.

Illustration showing the interior of a cathode-ray tube for use in an oscilloscope. Numbers in the picture indicate: 1. Deflection voltage electrode; 2. Electron gun; 3. Electron beam; 4. Focusing coil; 5. Phosphor-coated inner side of the screen.

New Words

dealership ['di:ləʃip] n. 代理权,经销权
diagnostic [daiəg'nɔstik] adj. 诊断的；特征的
instrument ['instrumənt] n. 仪器，器械，工具
technician [tek'niʃən] n. 技术员，技师

scan [skæn] v. 细看，审视；扫描；浏览 n. 扫描
domestic [də'mestik] adj. 国内的；家(庭)的，家用的
kit [kit] n. 成套工具(用品)；配套元件 v. 装备

adapter [ə'dæptə(r)] n. 适配器
graph [grɑ:f] n. 图表,曲线图
dashboard ['dæʃbɔ:d] n. (汽车上的)仪表盘
alignment [ə'lainmənt] n. 对准,校直,调整
specification [spesifi'keiʃən] n. 规格,详述,详细说明书

mileage ['mailidʒ] n. 里程,英里数
oscillograph [ɔ'siləgrɑ:f] n. 示波器
electromagnetic [ilektrəu'mægnitik] adj. 电磁的
momentum [məu'mentəm] n. 动力,冲力,势头;动量

Expressions

1. wheel alignment 车轮定位仪
2. electric current 电流
3. two-dimensional 二维的
4. cathode ray tube 阴极射线管
5. LCD screen 液晶显示屏
6. LED screen 二极管显示屏
7. analog-to-digital converter 模拟数字转换器

Notes on the Text

1. Due to the increasingly complicated nature of the technology that is now incorporated into automobiles, most automobile dealerships now provide sophisticated diagnostic computers and various instruments to each technician, without which they would be unable to diagnose or repair a vehicle.

因为汽车所含技术不断增长的复杂性,现在大部分汽车经销商给技术人员提供精密的诊断电脑和各种工具,没有这些设备辅助,他们将不能诊断或维修汽车。这些设备款式、品牌不一。

due to 意为"因为……",用法相当于because of。that is now incorporated into automobiles为定语从句,先行词为the technology。which they would be unable to diagnose or repair a vehicle也为定语从句,which指代computers and instruments。

2. A wheel alignment is part of standard automobile maintenance that consists of adjusting the angles of the wheels so that they are set to the car maker's specification.

车轮定位是常规汽车维护的一部分,它包括调整车轮角度使他们符合汽车制造规格。

句中that consists of adjusting the angles of the wheels为定语从句，先行词为maintenance；so that引导目的状语从句。

3. An oscilloscope (commonly abbreviated to scope or O-scope) is a type of electronic test instrument that allows signal voltages to be viewed usually as a two-dimensional graph of one or more electrical potential differences (vertical axis) plotted as a function of time or of some other voltage (horizontal axis).

示波仪（通常缩写为示波器或O-示波器）是一种能显示电压信号的电子设备测试仪，通常有二维图表显示一个或多个电位差异（垂直轴）以及时间功能或其他电压（水平轴）。

句中that allows signal voltages...为定语从句，先行词为instrument。view... as意为"当作……，认为是……"。

Exercises

1. Fill in the blanks with the suitable terms according to the text.

| repair | dashboard | suspension | dealership | alignment |
| parallel | fuel | maximum | oscillograph | tire |

(1) Most automobile _____s now provide sophisticated diagnostic computers and various instruments to each technician, without which they would be unable to diagnose or repair a vehicle.

(2) An _____ is an instrument for measuring alternating or varying electric current in terms of current and voltage.

(3) Plug your scan tool into the standard connector under the driver's side _____.

(4) The purpose of these adjustments is _____ tire life.

(5) Improper alignment is a major cause of premature _____ wear, while properly aligned vehicle can add thousands of miles to tire life.

(6) _____ mileage increases as rolling resistance decreases.

(7) Total alignment sets all four wheel _____ which minimizes rolling resistance.

(8) Many handling problems can be corrected by total _____.

(9) A _____ system inspection is part of alignment procedure.

(10) Without these instruments they would be unable to diagnose or _____ a vehicle.

2. Complete the following sentences with the words and phrases from the passage.

(1) A _____ is part of standard automobile maintenance that consists of adjusting the angles of the wheels so that they are set to the car maker's specification.

(2) An _____ (commonly abbreviated to scope or O-scope) is a type of electronic test instrument that allows signal voltages to be viewed, usually as a two-_____ graph of one or more electrical potential differences (vertical axis) plotted as a function of time or of some other voltage (_____ axis).

(3) An electromagnetic oscillograph is an _____ which measures variations of electric _____ by having it go through a magnetic coil. Variations in current induce _____ in the coil, which can be directly measured.

(4) Originally all oscilloscopes used _____ as their display element and linear amplifiers for signal processing, but modern oscilloscopes can have _____ or LED screens, high-speed analog-to-digital converters and digital signal processors.

3. Match the following English phrases in column A the Chinese equivalents in Column B.

A	B
wheel alignment	液晶显示屏
dashboard	车轮定位仪
electric current	示波仪
electromagnetic	电流
electromagnetic	电磁
LCD screen	仪表盘

4. Translate the following passages into Chinese.

(1) Most automobile dealerships now provide sophisticated diagnostic computers and various instruments to each technician, without which they would be unable to diagnose or repair a vehicle.
_____

(2) Plug your scan tool into the standard connector under the driver's side dashboard.
_____

(3) The purpose of these adjustments is maximum tire life.
_____

(4) An oscillograph is an instrument for measuring alternating or varying electric current in terms of current and voltage.
_____

5. **Training center practice:**

(1) In a training center, in front of a real engine, students are required to recognize the different maintenance instruments;

(2) Students are required to handle these instruments based on English instruction.

课文译文

汽车维修（Ⅱ）

因为汽车所含技术不断增长的复杂性，现在大部分汽车经销商给技术人员提供精密的诊断电脑和各种工具，没有这些设备辅助，他们将不能诊断或维修汽车。这些设备款式品牌不一。例如，OTC，因其诊断工具而闻名，它是汽车电子诊断设备、汽车燃油系统维护设备、特殊服务工具和万用工具等的主要生产和供应商。

下面粗略地介绍一下汽车维修的主要工具。

汽车扫描工具

因为使用简单，汽车扫描工具在汽车维修中广泛使用。这里有几种样品：

有彩色显示屏的USA 2007家用扫描工具箱，包括车身和底盘系统范围以及发动机、变速器、ABS和气囊。其他特征包括维修信息等。

特点

- 新——彩色显示屏
- 新——USB插口和电脑数据线
- 国产和亚洲车辆加强数据
- 不需要适配器
- 数据图解
- 记录和回放功能
- 适用于汽油和柴油机
- 自动记录数据
- 网络升级

车轮定位

车轮定位是常规汽车维护的一部分，它包括调整车轮角度使他们符合汽车制造规格。

降低轮胎磨损：调整的目的是达到车轮的最大使用寿命。不恰当的定位是车轮提前磨损的主要原因，而正确定位的车辆能使车轮增加几千英里的寿命。**更好的燃油里程数**：当车轮旋转阻力降低时燃油里程数会增加。完全的定位使车轮平行，使旋转阻力降低到最低。**改善操作**：全定位能校正很多的操作问题。所有的系统部件正确校直时，会更有效地减振，使驾驶更平稳。**驾驶更安全**：底盘系统检查是校直程序的一部分，这会使我们在它们产生问题之前检查出磨损部分。

示波器

示波器是以电流和电压的形式来测量交替或变化的电流的工具。示波器（通常缩写为示波器或O-示波器）是一种能显示电压信号的电子设备测试仪，通常有二维图表显示一个或多个电位差异（垂直轴）以及时间功能或其他电压（水平轴）。有两种示波器我们经常使用：

● 电磁示波仪：电磁示波仪是通过电磁线圈测量电流变化示波仪。电流的变化引起电磁的动量变化，可以被测到。

● 阴极射线示波仪：早先所有的示波器都用阴极射线管作为显示元件和线性放大器来处理信号，但是现在的示波器也有液晶或二极管显示屏，高速模拟-数字转换器和数字信号处理。